Shops that
POP!

D1089300

Shops that
POP!

7 Steps to
Extraordinary
Retail Success

PAMELA N. DANZIGER

with

Jennifer Patterson Lorenzetti

Paramount Market Publishing, Inc.

Paramount Market Publishing, Inc.
274 North Goodman Street, STE D-214
Rochester, NY 14607
www.paramountbooks.com
Voice: 607-275-8100

Publisher: James Madden
Editorial Director: Doris Walsh

Copyright © 2017 Pamela N. Danziger & Jennifer Patterson Lorenzetti
Printed in USA

All rights reserved. No part of this book may be reproduced,
stored in a retrieval system, or transmitted in any form or by
any means, electronic, mechanical, photocopying, recording,
or otherwise, without the prior written permission of the
publisher. Further information may be obtained from Paramount
Market Publishing, Inc., 274 North Goodman Street, STE D-214,
Rochester, NY 14607.

This publication is designed to provide accurate and authoritative
information in regard to the subject matter covered. It is sold
with the understanding that the publisher is not engaged in
rendering legal, accounting, or other professional services. If legal
advice or other expert assistance is required, the services of a
competent professional should be sought.

All trademarks are the property of their respective companies.

Cataloging in Publication Data available
ISBN-10: 01-941688-41-1 | ISBN-13: 978-1-941688-41-0 paper
eISBN-13: 978-1-941688-42-7

For all the retail "Davids"
who each day must
fight the growing legion of
national retailing "Goliaths"—

Good "Luxe"

Contents

Small Is the Next BIG Story in Retail

"We may affirm absolutely that nothing great in the world has been accomplished without passion."
—Georg Wilhelm Friedrich Hegel

Congratulations! If you operate an independent retail store that has survived the Great Recession, or even if you have opened such a store since the official end of the recession in June 2009, you are in the sweet spot of the consumer retail economy for at least the next decade. The next big story for retail will be small, as in small independent retail businesses.

Shopping malls are increasingly turning into ghost towns. Since 2010, more than two dozen enclosed shopping malls have closed, and an additional 60 are on the brink. By 2025, an estimated 15 percent or more of malls will be closed or repurposed, according to projections by Green Street Advisors. While mall owners blame the trend on the closing of anchor stores, like Macy's, JC Penney and Sears, the real reason behind the demise of malls is that shoppers have lost interest.

Today, the sameness and ubiquity of the big-box store experience is beginning to show fatigue. Walk through any of the nation's 1,000 or so enclosed malls and you might notice they all look much the same. Filled with the same stores offering the same merchandise at the same sale price, it's too much of the same thing. Consumers are beginning to look for something new and different and finding it on Main Street, not in the malls.

Shoppers Are Abandoning Malls and Coming Back to Main Street

Main Streets and the independent retailers that thrive there are on the cutting edge of a shift in retailing. While the Great Recession took out a wide swath of retailers – economic natural selection at work – the successful retailers that remain represent, by and large, the best and brightest. They have come through the worst and emerged onto the other side stronger, smarter, and more resilient.

This emerging retailing trend, fueled by the desire of the highest-potential and highest-spending customers' passion for a new shopping experience that they can't find at the mall, will reshape the retail landscape over the next decade. Specifically, demographic shifts, with both aging Baby Boomers and young Millennials looking for a more personal shopping experience, as well as heightened expectations from affluent consumers will favor the special services and products that only local small businesses can provide.

Customers will seek these smaller stores for different reasons, based on their demographic, socio-economic, and psychographic outlooks. As a result, growth at mass retailers will slow down and profits will shrink. The next decade will see a great winnowing down, restructuring, and rightsizing of mass-market retail, which will give a new opportunity to independent specialty retailers.

The secret of success for inspired, creative independent specialty retailers to prosper is the ability for them to really know their customers and deliver the valuable, unique shopping experiences these demanding, savvy, eager-to-be-pleased consumers crave. *Shops that POP! 7 Steps to Extraordinary Retail Success* is a book about and for independent specialty retailers who want to thrive in this new shopping environment.

Customers today demand a true "customer-centric" retailing experience, not in words as many big retailers do, but in reality, like today's specialty independent retailers do by necessity and design.

The Challenge of Independence

Running an independent retailing business is brutal. The faint of heart need not apply. The skill sets required for success are staggering. Retailers must have operational and management expertise, plus money management and budgeting skills, marketing and sales expertise, and technology savvy. Retailers must be trend forecasters, economists, masters of product display, and graphic artists. Most importantly, they need to have the expert people skills of a psychologist. All this, plus retailers need deep personal reserves of emotional and physical energy.

Specialty independent retailers face formidable day-to-day business challenges. The costs of doing business are extremely high and profits are hard to come by. The business of independents is also unforgiving. A retailer that makes just one simple mistake, such as picking a less than ideal location, making a poor hiring choice, or using a less-than-optimum marketing strategy, could be on the path to business closure.

Not only is an independent retailer's business environment challenging, but also bigger and better capitalized competitors are everywhere ready to give the small business a death blow. And then there are macroeconomic forces that hang over every retailer's business. With the pain of the Great Recession fresh in everyone's memory, along with the very slow, weak recovery, small independent retailers may rise and fall based upon economic forces over which they have no control and never will.

But despite these challenges, independent retailers have hope. They have something important and meaningful to share with the world, and their potential customers. They are compelled to bring that vision of their businesses and what they offer their customers to reality. The retailer's vision is important to them, to their customers, and to the world, and they will put it out there because they simply must.

That passion, that drive, that overwhelming need to give something great and important to the world is the ultimate secret of an independent retailer's success.

Independence Is a Huge Competitive Advantage

Today's consumer culture is turning to favor locally owned, independent retailers who contribute to the community. People recognize that Main Street businesses create jobs. The American Express-sponsored Small Business Saturday and the growing made-in-America movements all support the concept of buying from small independent retailers, rather than from big national chains. It's largely due to the recession that this new positive environment for independent specialty retail has emerged.

During and immediately following the recession, big national retailers prospered by offering shoppers lower prices. The U.S. Census Bureau's Economic Census is conducted every five years with the latest covering the years immediately before (2007) and after (2012) the recession. The census showed that the total number of retailers in operation dropped nearly 6 percent from 2007 to 2012. While the number of retailers declined, retail sales grew by nearly 8 percent in the same period. That means one thing: Retail sales became concentrated across a narrower band of larger retailers.

With few exceptions, most categories in retail experienced a sharp drop in number of establishments since 2007. Further, those segments of specialty retail traditionally dominated by independent retailers experienced the greatest decline. For example, the number of florists, art dealers, stationers, home furnishings stores, luggage and leather goods stores, gift and souvenir shops, and furniture stores all lost 20 percent or more doors in the five years from 2007 to 2012.

Today, independent specialty retailers are the antidote to the nation's growing homogenized retail landscape. Surely, the recession winnowed out many weaker and less competitive independents. But as in a garden, where thinning out the weaker shoots creates a nurturing environment so the stronger plants can reach their full potential, today's retail environment is ripe for inspired and creative independent specialty retailers to prosper. There is an emerging new retail marketplace where small is beautiful and independents attract a growing customer base looking for shopping experiences that are different, distinctive, and fun.

With a focus on research, both among shoppers and specialty independent retailers, *Shops that POP!* examines key factors that will translate into success and growth for independents. Through consumer research we focus on the shopping experiences that create loyalty among shoppers. We also study specialty independent retailers where people love to shop and what makes those store experiences so special.

You'll meet specialty retailers that share a set of unique identifying characteristics that make these extraordinary stores shops that POP! Specialty independent retailers who will inspire you include Charleston, South Carolina's Tiger Lily florist; Atlanta's Boxwoods Gardens & Gifts; Atchison, Kansas's Nell Hill's home specialty store; and Kermit's Key West Key Lime Shoppe. These stores share specific attributes, called the POP! Equation, that result in people loving to shop in them.

Throughout the pages of this book, you will learn more about the motivations, desires, and passions of shoppers; the characteristics of stores that evoke passion in their shoppers; and how to put these insights to work to transform your store into a retail experience that shoppers will love.

Success in Retailing: It's Not about What You Sell, but How You Sell It

"He liked to like people, therefore people liked him."
—Mark Twain

What makes people love shopping in shops that POP!, and what makes them passionate about the shopping experience, is that the store, in a very real sense, loves the shoppers back. By that we mean the retailer is passionate about delighting the customer. The staff shows a passion for the shoppers in the way they serve them and care for them. The design of the store shows passion for the shoppers' pleasure. The merchandise selection shows it. Shops that POP! offer extraordinary shopping experiences and they are also the ones that are truly consumer-centric in all aspects of their operations.

Shoppers reward these consumer-centric Shops that POP! with a passion that is overwhelming. They love to shop there, so they shop more often, spend more time in the store, and as a result spend more money. They love to tell their friends about shopping

there, so they become retail store evangelists sending out powerful word of mouth messages that entice more people
to shop in the store. It is viral marketing of the retail
variety. Success at retail is less about the product and
more about the shopping experience.

! Success at retail is less
about the product
and more about the
shopping experience.

It is important to understand that shoppers today focus on the
total shopping experience. They don't love a store simply because
they love the merchandise it carries. They love a store because it
touches them personally and emotionally. Surely they connect with
the merchandise, but what really evokes passion is the retailing
experience.

This shift in shopping away from a focus on product toward
the shopping experience marks the biggest change to occur in the
retailing landscape over the past century. As a result, retailing isn't
primarily a products-based business, but a people business that
creates shopping experiences for the consumer, with the objective
of selling stuff purely as the end result of that experience.

Ultimately, success at retail is less about *what* the retailer has to
sell and more about *how* they sell it. Because of this shift toward
the shopping experience, retailers' success is far less about product,
place/location, or price and all about the intangibles that color and
flavor the shopper's experience in the store. In order to be successful
a retailer must offer an enhanced, truly memorable, and distinctive
shopping experience to its customers.

The POP! Equation – The 7 Steps to Creating a Shop that POPs!

Retail will continue to be transformed toward an emphasis on
entirely new kinds of shopping experiences, which independent
specialty retailers are uniquely qualified to meet. The POP! Equation
is seven steps that transform a store from a place to buy things into
a place where shoppers find new and extraordinary experiences,
along with wonderful products to buy. It is a seven-step plan that
retailers mix together to make their stores, their shops, POP!

Let's meet one of them now: Godfrey's–Welcome to Dogdom,
an independent shop that is so electric that it exerts a magnetic
pull that draws shoppers who are passionate about their pets into
this boutique dedicated to the canine lifestyle.

Godfrey's – Welcome to Dogdom:
Godfrey's is so much more than just a store

Officially classified as a pet and pet supply store, Godfrey's – Welcome to Dogdom ranks among the few retail segments that experienced both growth in numbers (8,782 U.S. establishments in 2007 and 8,793 in 2012) and revenues ($11.4 billion in 2007 to $14.7 billion in 2012, a 29 percent increase) during the recession. However, Barb Emmett, owner of Godfrey's, doesn't credit being part of a hot retailing trend for the success of her destination boutique and lifestyle center that opened in July 2004. It's her passion for pets and a deep need to share it with other pet parents.

Godfrey's official mission is:

> My vision was to make Godfrey's the place for all of us who love dogs to celebrate the dogs in our lives. To create a beautiful, yet comfortable environment where fellow dog lovers could shop for high-quality, unique dog-themed items to make them smile and to make their dogs smile, too (yes, they really do smile!). To be a place where dog parents could buy super premium dog foods, holistic supplements and healthy treats, share stories with others, attend events with their dogs, and have fun!

Barb credits her store's year-over-year success to the fact that she knows who she is and what she values and she makes sure her store Godfrey's stays true to those values. "You are not selling product, you are selling experience. You got to get to the soul. I can't compromise my values. I have to be true to myself," she says. Barb takes a holistic approach to help pet owners engender happy, healthy lives with their pets. She is as much counselor and psychologist as retailer and merchandiser. "We are so much more than a store," she says. "We are a safe place for people to talk about their dogs, ask questions and get answers. It may not be a product necessarily, but they need help that day and they are telling us something. When they walk out that door, they feel like a weight has been lifted. You can see it."

Besides providing healthful food, treats, dietary supplements, pet supplies, dog-themed gifts and décor, Godfrey's offers two off-leash dog parks and membership play groups; nutritional counseling; wellness clinics; training classes; and a series of workshops devoted to educating pet parents and improving pet lives. As the company's tagline reads, "If you love dogs, you'll love Godfrey's . . . we're so much more than a canine store!"

Yet Barb faces challenges. Very simply, all that counseling, all that sharing, all that communicating of information and knowledge that she gives to her customers is not always "monetized." She explains, "You can't turn all that energy you put into it into dollars. The economy is changing. People are looking at prices on the internet. For example, we helped a customer with food allergies through our food nutritional analysis process. We gave them a solution and they were happy and came back once, but then I didn't see them again until I ran into them at the grocery store. They thanked me and told me how their dog had completely turned around. But they said, 'I'm ordering online.' Here we gave them solutions, so how can they go online? Generally it isn't even cheaper. But the world is so competitive, it is hard to figure out how to get loyalty. Our passion is getting healthier, happier dogs, that is what we do. So I have to let that go. But it's hard."

Growing out of her experience and services focus, Barb has made special events a core of her retail marketing. Leading up to Christmas, "Santa Paws" visits each Saturday in December to give treats. In the fall there is "Howloween" Trick or Treat, and spring brings the Easter Egg and Bone Hunt event.

Godfrey's also hosts recurring events including pet photography and workshops offered by a professional artist so customers can learn how to paint their pet. Barb promotes these events through Facebook postings, her website, and customer newsletters, but she finds the local newspaper's free weekend listing of upcoming events to be one of the best performers. "It's free and it works. People get that section and keep it around to find things to do all weekend. It sure beats spending $500 on an ad for one day, " she says.

Barb taps her vast store of pet research and experience to communicate with local pet parents that share her passion. In marketing terminology this is called "content marketing." She hosts a monthly local cable television show entitled "Dog Is Family." After being "discovered" by guesting on a local travel show, she worked with the station to create a proposal and two pilot shows. She was off. "The show is done live and I bring in guests," Barb explains. "It airs live on Thursdays, then plays several other times until it goes into the archives. The cable channel doesn't have statistics about how many people are watching, but I hear from people that they saw it when flipping through channels." Barb also does a weekly radio "Pet of the Week" spot on local radio featuring a dog available for adoption. "I make up my own spots. I want my voice to be the commercial, to make it personal, so I am seen as a community resource."

In a new content marketing initiative, Barb is writing a column for a limited circulation magazine that will be distributed to householders in a local affluent community. Instead of just advertising in each issue, Barb negotiated a deal to write a pet column to accompany her ad. "I didn't want just to pay for advertising. I wanted to make more of an impression, so my first article is about raising a healthy happy dog. It is all part of my 'Dog Is Family' brand," Barb says. The results of this effort aren't in yet, but Barb is building a library of information content that can be repurposed and disseminated in new and different ways. She trusts that this content will continue to give a return on her investment.

For the future Barb will continue to focus on customer service and pet/parent experiences to keep customers coming back. "It's not about what's on the shelves. It's about adding energy, service, heart."

Godfrey's – Welcome to Dogdom illustrates the seven key customer touchpoints that are the POP! Equation:

Involvement Godfrey's invites dogs to bring their parents to the store to shop, play and train. High involvement in all aspects of the pets' and their parents' lives is key.

Curiosity Godfrey's is off-the-beaten path for a reason: Its country location provides a safe play environment for the dog parks. Marketing outreach through information content create curiosity to come and see all that Godfrey's has to offer pets and their parents.

Contagion Friends-tell-a-friend is built into what Godfrey's is all about. Dogs are pack animals and so dog parents run in packs, too.

Convergence Godfrey's is located in an old Pennsylvania barn converted into a residence that now operates as a store. The central entrance is where the cash wrap desk is located. The living room houses gift and jewelry items, along with comfortable seating. Walk through the living room to the kitchen for food, while the bedrooms display pet supplies, collars, leashes, bedding and coats and the bath is where to go for bathing supplies. The homey atmosphere creates a comfortable environment for shoppers to interact with the merchandise and staff. Plus, there is always a friendly dog greeter on hand to welcome shoppers. Godfrey's is named for the store's first official greeter, Jackson Godfrey.

Authenticity Godfrey's is all about pets and Barb Emmett and her staff know, understand and live the pet-is-family lifestyle.

Price/value Godfrey's offers exceptional high-quality products, including the best quality food and supplements. Godfrey's doesn't sell the mass-market brands found in supermarkets or the national pet supply stores. Its products are definitively better and priced accordingly. But the value is there and customers can feel confident they are getting the best.

Accessibility Everyone is welcome at Godfrey's, even cat lovers, for Godfrey's also sells high-quality cat foods. But since cats aren't particularly social animals, Godfrey's in-store experiences and grooming, training and play services focus on dogs.

What's to Come

Shops that POP! is organized into three parts:

Part 1. The Customer Connection: Marketing Starts with Understanding the Customer.

Part 2. Retailing Stars: Secret Sauce that Turns an Ordinary Store into a Shop that POPs!

Part 3. Putting the POP! Equation to Work: Principles You Can Use to Make Yours a Shop that POPs!

Chapter 1

Today's Shoppers Crave New Shopping Experiences

"We are turning from a mass market back into a niche nation, defined now not by our geography, but by our interests."

—Chris Anderson

Retail experts Robin Lewis and Michael Dart in their book, *The New Rules of Retail: Competing in the World's Toughest Marketplace*, look at retailing across its 150-year evolution. The history of retail starts in 1850 and its first Wave, called "Producer Power" by Lewis and Dart, continued through about 1950. In the first wave of retail, consumer demand was greater than supply and distribution of goods was limited. Then came Wave II, 1950–2010, when tremendous economic growth brought about a massive expansion of products, along with retail and brand growth. In Wave II, retailers' challenge was to "Create Demand" for all those new products.

Today we are in Wave III, which they tell us is retail's greatest transformation yet. They write:

As companies battle for market share, consumers have grown accustomed to an instantaneous and unlimited selection of virtually anything they might dream of. This dynamic has led to their demand for experiences over 'stuff,' customized products and services over mass-market or 'mega' brands, real value over ostentatious 'bling,' constant novelty, immediate availability and, finally, product providers whose community interests and involvement trump their self-interest.

It is into this next, new wave of retail that independent retailers have a distinct competitive advantage, like Grapevine Farms in Cobleskill, New York.

Grapevine Farms Welcomes Its Customers Home

When Tracy Purcell and her husband, Tim, purchased an abandoned 1850s farmhouse, they couldn't have dreamed of the guests who would soon come to enjoy lunch, wine, dessert, and some of the most unique shopping in the area. But that's just what they created when they founded Grapevine Farms, a three-story country store and bistro rolled into one. Located between the Catskill and Adirondack Mountains, it attracts a passionate band of local customers, as well as being a destination to the many visitors to the area.

Visitors entering Grapevine Farms are struck by its home-like atmosphere, something that is created in part by the structure of the building but essential to the design of the store's experience. "There's a different feeling here, like walking into someone's house," Tracy Purcell says. Each room in the house has its own theme, allowing shoppers to transition seamlessly from a candle room to a jewelry room to rooms featuring items for kitchen and for baby and in the cellar, a wide selection of New York State wines. The front room contains a rotating seasonal display of items, and Purcell notes that it is not uncommon for her to sell all of her Christmas stock early when it is featured in this entry room.

Tracy isn't afraid to step outside her comfort zone to try new things that may fail. She notes that she resisted carrying jewelry brand ALEX AND ANI for a long time before giving the product line a try. It is now her number two brand behind Vera Bradley, both of which have an avid collector following and drive regular visits for customers to see what's new and different.

The heart of a home is the kitchen, so Grapevine Farms makes the comfort of good food an essential part of its charm. The full-feature Farmhouse Bistro came about experimentally when Tracy's husband wanted to bake cookies in the store to give it a welcoming aroma reminiscent of hearth and home. This quickly evolved into serving sandwiches and soup at lunch time on tables that at the time could seat only eight people. When the Purcells added onto the house, doubling its size, they included a commercial kitchen, wine cellar, and seating area for 48. Today, they serve lunch, coffee, and homemade ice cream, as well as hosting special events like baby showers, birthdays, and anniversary parties. The Farmhouse Bistro Chicken Salad Sandwich is a particular customer favorite, the fame of which got them invited to the 2014 World Food Championships in Las Vegas. "But we still make our own homemade cookies," Tracy says.

This dual focus on specialty retail and restaurant makes Grapevine Farms a destination for many of its visitors. "Some customers come just to eat lunch, some come and spend the day," Tracy says. The destination nature of Grapevine Farms has made word of mouth an important form of advertising for the store, although, in recent years, social media has also become an important way of reaching out with more than 15,000 likes on their Facebook page.

It is this willingness to experiment – with product lines and with homemade cookies – that has made Grapevine Farms a shop that POPs! "You have to be a little bit crazy," Tracy concludes.

Specialty Independent Retailers Must Be Crazy Like a Fox

Maybe it's a bit "crazy" to think opening a specialty retail store is a way to make a living in today's extremely challenging retail climate. With headlines like this one from CNBC, "A 'tsunami' of store closings expected to hit retail," and recent announcements from Sears, JC Penny, and Macy's about massive store closings, retail looks to be the last place anyone sane would want to be. And if we are talking mass-market retail, the next ten or so years are going to see a great winnowing down, restructuring, and rightsizing that will mean many more stores and malls will fold.

But that is at the mass-market level, not in small specialty segments of retail where independents can thrive as customers abandon the one-size-fits-all approach of mass-retail and seek out shopping experiences that are customized to their personal needs and desires.

Chris Anderson, author of *The Long Tail: Why the Future of Business Is Selling Less of More* explains:

> The theory of the Long Tail is that our culture and economy is increasingly shifting away from a focus on a relatively small

number of "hits" (mainstream products and markets) at the head of the demand curve and toward a huge number of niches in the tail. As the costs of production and distribution fall, especially online, there is now less need to lump products and consumers into one-size-fits-all containers. In an era without the constraints of physical shelf space and other bottlenecks of distribution, narrowly-targeted goods and services can be as economically attractive as mainstream fare.

The secret of success in the emerging niche of specialty independent retail is the ability for retailers to know – really know – their customers and deliver to them the special, unique shopping experiences they crave, which includes products, but a whole lot more. It is the secret that Godfrey's–Welcome to Dogdom and Grapevine Farms understand and you will too as we meet other shops that POP!

Specialty Independent Retailers
Know Their Customers Personally

Jim Blasingame, the small business advocate, sees the "long tail" trends that will favor small retailing as rooted in the customer now taking control of the relationship between buyers and sellers. In a change from the past, today the buyer is in charge.

Jim explains in his book, *The Age of the Customer: Prepare for the Moment of Relevance,* that the rules of marketing have shifted because of the transfer of power away from the traditional model where the seller largely controlled the information about the goods for sale through carefully-crafted advertising and other market-er-generated messages. He writes:

> The age of the customer is upon us. After centuries of markets driven in large part by those who sell, today's competitive environment is driven by the customer. This means marketers can't go forward with their marketing plans without deep consumer insights about motivations, not just behavior or demographics.

Where once the seller controlled the message, now product information is overwhelmingly crafted and created by the customer in User-Generated-Content (UGC) distributed via the internet and social media.

Customers can go to the internet for a rapidly expanding library of information about products and services. This has turned the tables on the marketer, with a resulting loss of power in their relationship with the customer. But specialty independent retailers can claim back some of that power by delivering a personalized experience. For example, a shopper can buy a Vera Bradley bag or an ALEX AND ANI bracelet almost anywhere without even venturing from home, but it isn't the fact that Grapevine Farms sells these brands that draws customers.

It is that they want the whole experience that comes when they visit and shop at Grapevine Farms. So, in a real sense, the product itself is transformed into a memory of the shopping experience. Every time they wear that bracelet or carry that bag, they are reminded of the warm feeling and the comforting experience they got when they visited Grapevine Farms. The real drawing power for the seller, in this case Grapevine Farms, is not the product, but the unique experience, which can't be easily duplicated.

What Grapevine Farms has achieved is relevance by giving a meaningful experience to the customer. Relevance is achieved by communicating important, interesting information and experiences to the customer, which makes him or her take notice. And it is through their unique and special ability to be relevant to their customers that independent specialty retailers will prosper.

Already there are signs in the marketplace that the big national retailers are catching onto the need for relevance – that is, understanding the needs and desires of the customer and aligning business processes, product offerings, and service levels to those needs. In an effort to be more relevant, big-box retailers like Target and Walmart announced small-store initiatives for 2015. Luxury-leaning Bloomingdale's is doing the same thing, expanding its smaller-scale SoHo concept to affluent shopping centers in California and Washington, D.C. area.

Problem is, and the problem always will be, these big-box and mass merchandise retailers can reduce their store footprints in an effort to be relevant, but they can never achieve the true connection and relevance with their customers that an independently owned specialty retailer can. All the "big data" that these big retailers can collect and analyze about the customers will never replace that one-on-one personal interaction specialty retailers have day in and day out.

Big Retail Is Boring,
Small Retailing Is Interesting, Exciting, Inviting

Very simply the big national retailers, as much as they give lip service to customer service and connection, operate primarily a product-selling business and as Jim Blasingame stresses, product is no longer going to set a retailer apart. People can find good quality products at really attractive prices anywhere and everywhere. They only need to go to the store to get products if they want to. But with time increasingly precious, people don't need to waste it to buy a product. They can go online in a spare moment and have it delivered to the door.

Specialty retailers operate in a totally different realm of customer experiences that can be made relevant and personal for each customer because of the intimacy with customers that shop owners can engender. A study of retailing trends, entitled *Retailing 2015: New Frontiers,* by PricewaterhouseCoopers and TNS Retail, reports that a more indulgent consumer will increasingly seek out "niche products, experiences, and services uniquely suited to their tastes, interests and aspirations." This gives small independents a decided edge.

Mass merchandisers simply can't provide the niche products for narrow bands of customers. They have to and always will think big even in their small-format stores. That is because their financials require that product manufacturers deliver huge orders with minimums of 20,000 pieces. Mass marketed and merchandised products can't fulfill a customer who craves something unique and customized to his or her special tastes.

Demographic Shifts Will Favor Smaller, Local Stores

Demographic shifts will also favor small specialty retailers in the coming decade. The maturing of the huge Baby Boom generation, which will range in age from 56–74 years in 2020, will bring customers who are looking for more personal retailing experiences. They have gone through life stages of family formation and child rearing, which favored mass merchants, and acquired many of the material things that those life stages demanded.

Those customers are now in their empty nest years, characterized by a shift of spending toward experiences and preference for a slower, more local, and more personal shopping experience. The PricewaterhouseCoopers/TNS Retail report says, "As they approach age 70, First-Wave Baby Boomers will be reaching a lifestage where spending on many goods begins to decline. They will have new needs, driven by smaller households, increased emphasis on health and general welfare, and increased service demands as 'help me' replaces 'DIY.' They will have new requirements – smaller, closer, and easier. And they will have new desires, such as quality of life, experiences, entertainment, enrichment, leisure and legacies."

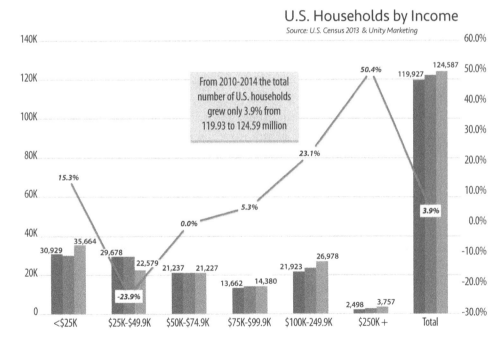

An increasingly affluent customer base also gives specialty independents an edge. The affluent, defined as those with household incomes in the top quintile, starts just slightly above $100,000 in today's market and is the fastest growing segment in the post-recession economy. In fact, the number of households at the very top of the income pyramid of $250,000 and above increased by 50 percent since 2010. These high-income households are the ones for which special, customized, niche, and exclusive products and shopping experiences in local shops are most attractive.

Affluent consumers have the discretionary incomes on which specialty independent retailers rely, for the goods they sell are not so much things people need, as things people desire. People buy the stuff they need at the mass-merchandisers and big boxes because that is where they are cheap; they buy the things they want, desire, even love, in small shops where they can share their passion with the store owners and staff.

For example, if people want to, or due to price have to, feed their dogs Purina or Alpo they go to Walmart or the grocery store. But if they want more specialized pet food not available at mass retailers, they go to independent specialty stores like Godfrey's–Welcome to Dogdom where they can get counseling on the best options for a special dog with special tastes. Not only that, they can bring their dog along on the shopping trip.

And Grapevine Farms doesn't thrive on selling stuff people need, for nobody *needs* anything they sell. Instead their customers crave the sensual experience of fine food, wine, and the atmosphere it delivers, along with the fun of finding something interesting and different to wear or decorate with.

Another specialty independent retailer understands the special-ness its customers require and even further views the products it sells not as merchandise, but as the plot elements of a story. And more importantly, it's the story itself that this shop sells; the product is only a part of the experience. Meet Rachel Shechtman, owner and founder of the STORY store in New York City.

STORY Is a Small Retailer that Thinks BIG!

At 2,000 square feet and one store front in the Chelsea area of Manhattan, STORY is by every measure a small independent retailer, but Rachel Shechtman thinks any way but small when it comes to her business. Indeed, her ideas of specialty retailing for the 21st century are quite revolutionary. She explains, "The past 20 years have been filled with non-stop digital and technological innovation, however in terms of retail, there is not a whole lot that's new beyond Apple. You have so many new business models online, and yet for physical retail, it's still all about sales per square foot. It's beyond archaic in my opinion."

Coming from a background in brand consulting with clients such as Bliss Spa, Gilt Group, and TOMS shoes, Rachel launched STORY as a store with the "Point of View of a Magazine, Changes Like a Gallery, Sells Things Like a Store," as its website, www.thisisstory. com, says.

Rachel explains, "A magazine tells stories between pictures and written words, and we do it through merchandising and events. And our version of publishing is sponsorship." Specifically, every four to eight weeks STORY is completely made over, with new merchandise to sell and new stories to tell, such as its Color STORY, Wellness STORY, Made in America STORY and for the 2014 holiday season, Home for the Holidays STORY in partnership with Target.

STORY's sponsorship arrangements, a new-age version of slotting fees, give brands the opportunity to tell their story to the hip, young, socially-engaged customers that STORY attracts. "Brands pay us to become part of the experience; their name is on the wall and we activate different opportunities within STORY that are customized around their objectives," Rachel says.

The Target story came about when a Target executive team, including CEO Brian Cornell, visited the store. Rachel, anything but a shrinking violet, introduced herself and the deal got done in less than eight weeks. The result: Target showcased nearly 200 different branded products from Target's holiday gift assortment in STORY, including new offerings by TOMS and Target exclusives from Archer Farms and interior designer Nate Berkus.

STORY's sponsorship fees range from $75,000 to $500,000, depending on the level of service, and major brands including General Electric, Benjamin Moore, American Express, Pepsi, and HP have gladly lined up to pay it to get face time with STORY's customers, who anxiously line up to see the next rotating exhibition.

Ultimately Rachel measures success in "experiences per square foot," rather than sales. Those experiences are measured in a revolutionary way. The STORY store is heat-mapped, which detects the movement of customers through the store and how long they stop to interact with specific product displays. This provides data that turns STORY into a live product research center where a sponsor can see precisely what products are hot, and which are not, by the measure of consumer engagement.

STORY is far less about the products it sells, and far more about creating unique and special customer experiences. Products tell the story, but they aren't *the* story. Rachel says, "We have to let our story drive the assortment, rather than let the assortment drive our story. And when that story is sincere, it will spread just like a viral video, attracting all demographic groups, from 9-year-old Bella, who lives up the street, to my 65-year-old neighbor."

That perspective makes STORY a shop that POPs! Rachel concludes, "This is a paradigm shift. I think that physical retail spaces will become more about community and entertainment, and less focused solely on consumption."

PART 1

The Customer Connection

Marketing Starts with
Understanding the Customer

Chapter 2

Why People **Shop** and Why People **Buy** Are Different

"I don't shop because I need something, I just shop for shopping's sake."

—Cat Deeley

The dynamics of shopping – (what moves people to engage in shopping) and the dynamics of buying (what moves people to put their money down to make a purchase) are two different things, though dependent upon each other. You can't get customers to buy until you get them to shop, to visit the store, open the catalog, or visit the website. For the retailer, the chief goal of attracting shoppers is to turn them into buyers.

Four Things Turn Shoppers into Buyers

Turning shoppers into buyers breaks down around four key factors that engage the shopper during the shopping cycle: Need, Product Features, Affordability, and Emotion.

Here Is How It Works

Need sets the shopper in motion. A person's need for something often starts the cycle in motion. Unity Marketing's Shopper Track surveys, which focus on the shopping behavior of the top 20 percent of households based on income, find that the need to find a specific item or to make a purchase is the number one factor in why people shopped most recently.

Product features attract attention. Once the need is felt and shoppers start the process, other tangible factors, such as product features and affordability, come into play. Starting with need, shoppers turn to look at what product features are most desired.

Affordability determines what it is worth. Once their attention is drawn to the products, price becomes an issue. Specifically, is it worth the price asked?

Emotions seal the deal. Following these tangible factors – need, features and affordability – comes emotion, which is the experiential component of how the needed/desired purchase will make one feel. Emotions color all the other factors and ultimately play the greatest role in turning the shopper into buyer.

For example, you are fresh out of milk, so you head out to the grocery store to grab a half-gallon. In the milk section you are confronted with a dizzying array of product choices – skim, whole, 2%, 1%, lactose-free, almond, soy – and brands.

Narrowing the scope of your product choices is price and affordability – how much is this or that product selection worth, $2.00, $3.50, $4.00? For some shoppers the greatest share of the purchase decision hinges on price, but for the affluent top 20 percent price usually is not dominant; rather, it typically is interpreted with an eye toward value. So you scan the options and prices and select Horizon Organic 1% low-fat priced for $3.99, higher than most other options on the shelf.

This is where emotions come into play. Surely, you could find a cheaper milk, but Horizon Organic is a brand that you have come to trust for its commitment to organic farming and its promise of 100 percent natural, wholesome milk with no additives. Because of this, you feel good bringing this milk brand home to your family.

Emotions magnify the need – you don't need to buy organic milk, but other commercially produced options aren't as healthy. Emotions guide your selection of features desired and they cause you to spend more money than absolutely necessary to get the combination of features that represent value in your world. Emotions magnify need, they play off features and they make a desired item more or less affordable, thus sending the shopper to the cash register with whatever it is they hunger for.

❗Emotions magnify need, they play off features to make a desired item seem more or less affordable.

As marketers and retailers we can control to some extent the tangibles, but not a whole lot. For example, consumer need is a very personal thing and no marketer or retailer can create the need for a particular item. Either you need a gallon of milk or you don't. No amount of advertising, marketing promotion, in-store advertising, or window displays can impact that personal need.

On the other hand, retailers can create desire, which is an emotional response. The key for the specialty retailer is how to turn the shopper's individual need into a desire for their more specialized, often higher-priced goods that will deliver positive emotions and create an emotional connection between the shop and the customer. That is what makes a shop POP!

Meet Mary Carol Garrity, owner of Nell Hill's. Her store, serving customers' home decorating needs and desires, plays off the key factors – need, product features and affordablity, but it is around emotion that she has built her business. Emotion is what draws the bulk of her customers more than 90 miles to shop.

Nell Hill's –
A Store in the Middle of Nowhere that Is Worth the Drive

An hour outside Kansas City, Missouri, in Atchison, Kansas – an unfathomable distance from a major city for the retail world – sits Nell Hill's home furnishings store. Owned by Mary Carol Garrity and her husband, Nell Hill's challenges the conventional wisdom that the key to success of a retail store is "location, location, location." Instead, over more than three decades, Garrity has grown her store to include two separate shops in Atchison, Kansas, and one in Briarcliff, Missouri, in locations that require the vast majority of its customers to drive between an hour and three hours to reach the store.

Founded in 1981, Nell Hill's has maintained success in spite of a retail environment that has grown ever-more challenging thanks to the recession. Mary Carol's secret is that her store is about more than just decorative home goods, "Decorating is just half of it," she says. Instead, she sells the experience of shopping in Nell Hill's. "Our goal is to be a wonderful experience that you can't get anywhere else or online," she says. This experience is one part accessibility and one part elegance.

Customers feel equally comfortable in Nell Hill's whether they have popped in wearing shorts or dressed up to make a day of it. The comfort comes from the warmth of the environment that encourages interaction with the merchandise. "It's not a museum; you can take something off the mantle or a coffee table," Mary Carol says. Staff members discretely come behind to reset the display, ensuring that the perfect vignette is always on view.

And customers will want to take careful note of those displays, because they won't be around for long and they reflect an expertly crafted style that many want to copy when they get back home. "You can come in every four weeks and see different vignettes on the floor," she says. "People will travel a good hour and a half to visit every couple of weeks because our merchandise changes so dramatically. There is a lot of energy going on here. People say, 'I can't believe how much everything has changed since the last time.'"

This merchandising strategy works to get products into the customers' hands and out the door. "People who shop here know that if they see it and want it, they had better buy it. It won't be here the next time they come," she says.

Mary Carol depends on a fleet of highly trained staff members to create the Nell Hill's experience. Not only does her staff perform the expected display-creation and sales-assistance duties, they also go the extra mile that makes a visit to Nell Hill's memorable. For example, Mary Carol refuses to have an office, but spends her time on the sales floor constantly rubbing shoulders with shoppers, learning their likes and preferences, and using those first-hand insights to drive all operating decisions.

Mary Carol also makes sure that a concierge is on duty, ready to provide driving directions, a lunch reservation, or assistance in finding a hotel for the night. The experience is memorable enough that Nell Hill's can rely on word of mouth as its most important form of advertising. "People come back and bring their sister, their mother, their girlfriend, or their spouse," she says.

But Mary Carol doesn't just sell great home decor, she lives and breathes it. Her merchandising strategy is simplicity itself. "We just buy stuff we love. Ninety percent of the things we have in our three stores, I would gladly have in my own home in a heartbeat." Her deeply personal touch doesn't go unnoticed by her enthusiastic customers, like this customer who drove 500 miles from the Chicago area to shop, "It's an amazing store. It's got a cozy feel, like you're shopping in a [private] home."

Of course, Nell Hill's can't compete effectively with the big-box stores without presenting a value proposition. Although Mary Carol describes her store as "medium- to high-end," she says her accessories line is affordably priced and comparable to a store like Home Goods. "You could spend $5 or $5,000 in Nell Hill's," she says. This wide range allows her to compete on price without becoming a discount store.

Weathering the recession was a challenge for Garrity. "You just have to have your game face on," she says. "I had just opened a new store when the stock market crashed; I was one nervous Nellie," she says. She survived by concentrating on what Nell Hill's is known for – a unique and memorable shopping experience.

"Retail is a tough way to earn a living," Mary Carol concludes, estimating that retail is second only to the challenges of running a restaurant. She credits the support of family and staff with Nell Hill's success. "You have to have the people you love supporting you," she says. Having this has allowed Mary Carol to spend her days on the magical sales floor of Nell Hill's, creating shopping experiences for all her customers. "I had to focus on what I did best," she says.

Chapter 3

Shoppers' Need
Transforming Desire Into Need

"We are driven by five genetic needs: survival, love and belonging, power, freedom, and fun."

—Psychiatrist Dr. William Glasser

Need Stimulates Shopping, While Desire Drives Purchases

Most people view shopping as both a chore and a recreational activity. In Unity Marketing's Shopper Track survey, about 40 percent of affluent shoppers surveyed say that shopping is "something that has to be done," a necessity in our lives. But nearly the same percentage, 38 percent, say that shopping can also be fun. People today seek fun to satisfy an emotional need, for escape, as a reward, to relax, to find excitement, for therapy. Nell Hill's, for example, makes "fun" the essential feature of the shopping environment. And STORY is all about recreational shopping, visiting the store to discover each new merchandising "story" it sells and to see the new products displayed.

Shops that POP! deliver satisfying and fulfilling emotional experiences first, since specialty retailers rarely sell products that their customers "strictly" need. Rather they specialize in products their customers desire – another emotional need state.

Justifiers Turn Desires Into Needs and
Give Shoppers Permission to Buy

Shoppers use justifiers to transform a desire into a need. It's a game of the mind, driven by emotions, and something a retailer can use to stimulate purchases. Retailers can tap the marketing power of justifiers to encourage people to buy.

Here are some of the justifiers that shoppers use that transform their personal desire into a real need:

Special occasion   A gift occasion or a special event can send shoppers to the store to buy. Marketers and retailers can play up the special occasion appeal of specific goods. This is important for gift destinations like Grapevine Farms; in fact, the visit itself becomes a special occasion. Special occasions and holidays can bring shoppers to the store, like Godfrey's and its Howloween doggie dress up event.

Beautify self or home   Things to make oneself or one's home beautiful give an emotional boost. Marketers and retailers need to display goods to maximize the beauty impact and send beautifying promises to consumers, like Mary Carol Garrity does at Nell Hill's.

Pleasure   Shoppers derive pleasure in the having, owning, and using, as well as in the buying. Anticipating a new purchase and searching out something wonderful can be part of the pleasure of shopping. Retailers and marketers need to maximize the pleasure in the shopping experience itself. It is for fun and pleasure that shoppers drive an hour to visit Nell Hill's. It's for fun people travel to Grapevine Farms to enjoy the atmosphere, drink a glass of wine and splurge on a new Christmas ornament. And fun is what brings dog owners out to Godfrey's every week. They take great joy in seeing their dogs romp in the play park with their "pack" friends.

> ❗ Justifiers are the reason, the rationale, the excuse, the *permission* to buy.

Education   Being better educated, more learned, and gaining new understanding and skills is an important motivator for the purchase of many categories of goods, notably home computers and peripherals, books, DVDs, and music and musical instruments. Improving one's education is a key way Americans achieve a higher standard of living. Barb Emmett of Godfrey's educates her customers on pet care, diet and exercise. STORY educates shoppers on what's new, what's hot, and what's important for them to know.

Relaxation and stress relief   Finding solace, relief from everyday stress, and achieving inner peace and harmony are favored motivators for buying many types of goods that offer an experiential value, like candles, aromatherapy, bath and body lotions, whirlpools, hot tubs, and others. Stress relief is delivered by the specific products, as well as the shopping experience itself. "Retail therapy" is real.

Entertainment   People crave entertainment to relieve boredom, and for the sheer enjoyment of doing something new and different. STORY is all about entertaining customers, bringing them together to share fun. This is a key justifier stimulating the purchase of many recreational and entertainment products. Shopping too can be an entertaining adventure.

Replacing a worn item   As the shopping adventure often starts with a practical purpose in mind, many shoppers are in the store specifically to replace an existing item. But this can also be a powerful motivator to move upscale to a more differentiated product or brand and to buy add-on items necessitated by a specific purpose. Nell Hill's creates little rooms and vignettes to encourage customers to buy not one item, but to take the whole scene home. So a shopper replacing a worn out chair also buys a new lamp, rug and curtains to match.

Emotional satisfaction   Many shoppers get pleasure from browsing, while others need to make a purchase to maximize their emotional satisfaction. Emotional satisfaction comes from finding that special something, or getting a really good deal, or just being authentically welcomed into the shop. Specialty retailers must play to the emotions of the shopper.

The Ultimate Justifier – Enriching One's Quality of Life

While a wide range of justifiers are used by consumers to give themselves permission to make purchases they otherwise don't need, the ultimate justifier that transforms wants into needs is how a particular purchase will enrich the quality of one's life. Enriching the quality of one's life can be measured objectively, like the greater comfort you get from 400-thread count Egyptian cotton sheets or the better sleep quality delivered by a luxury pillow-top mattress, but most often, it is measured subjectively, i.e., how it *promises* to make the customer feel.

This is what motivates consumers to improve their standard of living. It drives them to buy bigger houses, more expensive cars, more fashionable clothes, more up-to-date appliances, newer furniture, and all the rest. It is why we don't just stay where we are, but pursue aggressively the means to improve the quality of our lives.

Marketers and retailers need to position their products, merchandise their stores, and design the overall shopping environment to enhance the quality of the shoppers' lives. People want to buy the best item with the highest levels of quality and the most superior features that they can afford. Anyone who uses an OXO kitchen tool can immediately recognize its superior usability over the ordinary generic model. It is also why consumer product companies routinely reconfigure their products around the new and improved versions.

! Position your products, merchandise your stores, and design your shopping environment to enhance shoppers' quality of life.

Shoppers Need to Improve the Quality of Their Lives

The buying and getting of material goods today is directed mostly toward improving the quality of the shopper's life. True physical need – food, clothing, shelter – most often sends us to the store, but higher-level needs – improving the quality of life – directs spending.

Psychologist Abraham Maslow originally proposed a hierarchy of needs that give insight into how desires for an enhanced quality of life are transformed into personal needs. As each lower-level need is satisfied, people progress up to the next level.

Maslow's Hierarchy of Needs*

Physiological Needs Biological needs include oxygen, food, water, and a relatively constant body temperature.

* Derived from Abraham Maslow, *Toward a Psychology of Being,* 3rd edition (New York, John Wiley, 1998)

Safety Needs Safety needs have to do with establishing stability and consistency in a chaotic world. These needs are mostly psychological in nature. We need the security of a home and family, freedom from physical violence, crime, and so on.

Needs of Love, Affection, and Belongingness Love and belongingness are the next need in the hierarchy. Through the expression of these needs, people overcome feelings of loneliness and alienation.

Needs for Esteem There are two types of esteem needs. First is self-esteem, which results from competence or mastery of a task. Second, there is esteem that comes from the attention and recognition others give. Desire for status and the aspiration for status symbols, like expensive cars, are an expression of this need for esteem.

Needs for Self-Actualization The need for self-actualization is "the desire to become more and more what one is, to become everything that one is capable of becoming." People who have everything satisfied at the lower levels can realize their full human potential. They seek such things as knowledge, peace, aesthetic experiences, self-fulfillment, and oneness with God.

Because of the enormous material wealth present in our culture, most 21st-century Americans have satisfied the lower-level physical and safety needs as defined by Maslow. Shopping today can be linked in certain categories and under specific circumstances as a means to satisfy the love, affection, and belongingness need and the need for esteem. But more often, it is primarily a drive toward self-actualization.

As we look to the future of shopping and retailing, self-actualization will become the dominant motivator for our customers. Shoppers will buy goods and services that in some way offer the prospect of personal transformation, and of helping the individual create a new, more idealized self. It explains the pursuit of self-fulfillment through spiritual enlightenment, greater knowledge, peace, appreciation of beauty, culture, art, and aesthetics. It motivates consumers to develop hobbies, pastimes, exercise, and sporting activities that will lead to personal growth. It opens up an entirely new way to look at the world of shoppers – not just as people looking for more stuff to buy, but people in search of a new, more self-actualized self.

So the next time you welcome a shopper into your store or answer a phone call or email, think of this person not just as a potential customer, but as an individual in search of self-actualization and personal transformation. It opens up an entirely new way to look at the world of shoppers – not just people looking for more stuff to buy, but people in search of a new, more self-actualized self.

! It opens up an entirely new way to look at the world of shoppers – people in search of a new, more self-actualized self.

Help the customers transform themselves and you will build a loyal shopper who will return to your store again and again, because personal transformation is not a once-and-done thing, it is a perpetual, never-ending process.

Meet Dorothy Lane Market, a Local Grocer that Fulfills Self-Actualization through a Food Experience

Going to the grocery is not usually an uplifting experience, but it is when visiting one of the three Dorothy Lane Market locations in the Dayton, Ohio suburbs owned by Norman Mayne and family. DLM was founded as a roadside produce stand in 1948 by the current owner's father. But today its shoppers come away feeling somehow elevated, more self-actualized for the DLM shopping experience.

A closer look makes it easy to see why. A motto in Latin greets everyone who enters DLM, and sums up the Maynes' philosophy toward their customers, their staff, and the community, but it is not until you are leaving that the translation is revealed. It says, "Whatever is rightly done, however humble, is noble."

This motto sets the tone for the entire visit, as does the reception one receives when calling the store: staff answering the phone are unfailingly polite, and soft classical music plays during any hold time. Shoppers at DLM are not treated as faceless consumers as they sometimes are at big box grocers. Instead, DLM shoppers recognize the store as an important aspect of the luxury lifestyle they lead – or aspire to.

From the first interaction, the customer is treated as an intelligent, sophisticated person worthy of respect. The experience continues throughout the store, where customers find a deli department that is a lunch and dinner destination for many looking for a home-made-tasting meal that is healthy and prepared fresh. It includes a legendary bakery with its famous "Killer Brownie" that is a star at any meal, and a wide range of local, organic, and artisanal food choices stock the aisles. The visit is complete when a uniformed worker, probably a local high school or college student, bags your groceries and takes them to your car.

The heart of Dorothy Lane Market is the focus on "flavor first," says Jerry Post, store director of the Oakwood store. They lead with flavor because that is where they directly touch the customer and so enhance the quality of their food experiences. Jerry explains that the store has always prided itself on cooking in small batches to create a homemade taste in all of its deli items. This led to an experiment with cooking with organic ingredients, which was adopted throughout the stores when it brought a noticeable improvement in flavor. Any desire to return to conventional ingredients was rejected as taking an unacceptable toll on flavor. "If it doesn't taste right, it doesn't taste right," Jerry says.

The focus on flavor extends to provision of prime steaks, European-style breads, and, of course, the Killer Brownie. So popular are the Killer Brownies, along with other DLM baked goods, that area customers are proud to show up at dinners and parties with a box bearing the DLM logo, instead of trying to pass the product off as their own creation. Indeed, author and food celebrity Ree Drummond, "The Pioneer Woman," has written about her experience with the Killer Brownie and her unsuccessful attempts to replicate it at home.

Jerry attributes DLM's success to the team of young people pushing carts, stocking shelves, and ringing registers. These employees from the Millennial generation ensure that the store keeps moving forward, while still accommodating the core Baby Boom customer. "It's Millennials that are changing the market," Jerry says, crediting them with suggestions about how to get customers into the store to see the fresh products. Because of their input, the stores are partially designed around small displays and product stations, especially in the bakery, deli, and fresh produce departments.

Other areas of the store are, by necessity, displayed in traditional store aisles. "Thirty years ago, people used to spend four hours a week in the store [shopping for groceries]; today they spend one and a half," Jerry explains. This emphasis on speed means that stores like DLM have a limited amount of time to form relationships with their customers. Nonetheless, this personal touch is a core value at DLM, with staff getting to know regulars and their preferences. This behavior is echoed by the store owner, who typically knows nearly every one of his rotating staff of 800 by name.

Although DLM still encounters competition from larger area chains, particularly Cincinnati-based Kroger, Jerry believes that no one can match DLM's flavor or culture or customer experience. Although Kroger has made great strides to improve product quality through its Fresh Selections brand, the ambiance found in a large chain store cannot match the DLM shopping experience. Nor can Kroger compete with DLM's Culinary Center, which hosts a wide range of cooking classes with such popular offerings as couples cooking, cooking for kids, and opportunities for families to learn to cook together.

From the moment one sees that Latin tag line to when the groceries are loaded into the car, the shopping experience offers quality, an opportunity for individual expression, and even the opportunity to feel a bit ennobled. Not bad for a trip to the grocery store for some organic produce and Killer Brownies.

Chapter 4

Features

Added-Value Features
Touch Emotional Hot Buttons and
Compel Shoppers to Buy

"The aim of marketing is to know and understand the customer so well the product or service fits him and sells itself."

—Peter F. Drucker

Professor Brian Wansink is the most famous social scientist that you've probably never heard of, though you have undoubtedly been impacted by his research. His official title, the John Dyson Professor of Marketing and the Director of the Cornell Food and Brand Lab in the Department of Applied Economics and Management at Cornell University in Ithaca, New York, is quite long and his CV is even longer, with 31 pages listing his scholarly articles.

To the rest of us, Brian is known for his best-selling book, *Mindless Eating: Why We Eat More than We Think,* as well as the invention of the 100-calorie snack pack. He is also the brains behind the widespread use of taller glasses in bars and restaurants to prevent over pouring and over consumption of alcoholic beverages, the discovery that serving food on smaller plates leads to eating fewer calories, and research that has resulted in many chain restaurants spicing up their menu offerings with elaborate names and mouth-watering descriptions that both tempt the diner to spend more money and to enjoy the food more.

It is from this last discovery that retailers can learn much from Professor Wansink's work. Specifically, if we change the customer's perception of the product, we can change their behavior, i.e., they will buy more, and ultimately gain greater satisfaction from their purchase.

In Marketing, Perception Is Reality

Professor Wansink and his Cornell Food Lab set up an experiment to study the effects of people's perception on their overall enjoyment of food. The researchers went out to a local warehouse market and bought some packaged fish, green beans, scalloped potatoes, salad, and chocolate cake. Then they invited people in to eat the food, and that is when things got really interesting. One group was asked to sit at plain institutional tables, given a menu card that listed the food just as above, and were served their meal on paper plates. This "plain-Jane" group got only the basic meal with no ambiance. At the end, they were asked to rate the food served on a scale from 1 to 10, and they gave it an average rating of 3.4 points.

Another group was given an upscale restaurant dining experience. Their tables were set with linens with candles and a flower centerpiece. The room's lighting was lowered just like in a fine restaurant. This group's menu card gave a detailed, fancy food description of panko-encrusted Mediterranean sea bass fillet, sautéed French green beans, and the like. Their food was served on dinnerware plates, with restaurant-styled tableware and glasses. While the exact same food was served to this group as the other, their food was prettied-up on the plate, as one would expect in an upscale restaurant environment. When asked to rate the food, this group gave an average of 8 points on the same 10-point scale. What accounted for the difference? People's perception and expectation.

Change people's perception and expectation of the product and you change everything: what they'll buy, how much they'll spend, and how satisfied they will be with their purchase ultimately. Retailers, you have this kind of power at hand. The secret is to lead with the customer's experience, enhancing it, improving it, structuring it, and building it up, and you'll change how your customers experience the products you offer.

That is one reason we can expect that the sales of the exact same Target gift products offered in STORY during their Home for the Holidays presentation differed markedly from sales in the regular Target stores. No doubt, the executives at Target are puzzling over the differing sales results and trying to figure out how to replicate the STORY results across the entire chain of stores.

Specialty Retail Is a People Business First, Product Business Second

Too often specialty retailers hold the mistaken notion that product is the key to their success. But as the Wansink and Cornell Food Lab experiment shows, it's not the product first and foremost that drives sales and satisfaction; rather it is the way the product is perceived which then drives how it is experienced. Providing the right context for the product through the store's displays, creating ambiance, including lighting and sound, delivering superb customer service, and personal interaction can transform an ordinary product (a 3.4 on a 10 point scale) into an 8 (or even up to a 10, depending).

Specialty retailing is all about what's "special" and what's special must be seen, felt and perceived by the customer. Undoubtedly, product in and of itself plays a role, as people want a product experience when they shop, and they head out to the store due to a need, but in and of itself, product rarely is the secret of a retailer's success or the customers' satisfaction. Specialty retail is first and foremost a people, not a product, business. So retailers need to focus on the people side of the shopping experience, with product that supports the special shopping experience people have come to expect from your store. That is where success will be achieved.

! Specialty retail is first and foremost a **people**, not a product, business.

Products Must Be Special for Your Special Customers

If need causes people to shop, product features that make an item stand above the rest often turn that need into desire, which in turn transforms the shopper into a customer. Product features are those distinctive attributes, values, and qualities of an item or a brand that makes the shopper chose one item over another. It is what makes shoppers say, "I'll take this," at which point they become customers.

Product manufacturers and marketers tend to overemphasize the importance of product in why people shop and think that product, above all else, is the reason why people buy. Product features become important in so far as they create experiences for the shopper. It's all about the feelings and emotions that the products promise to deliver to the shopper.

Products Deliver Emotional Experiences – That Is the Meaning and Why People Buy Them

Ultimately, it is not the thing itself that people buy, but the promise of how that thing will perform emotionally and experientially for them. Too often we overlook the concept of product performance when it comes to things that primarily deliver an emotional response. By contrast, product performance is well understood when thinking about things that have gears and switches like cars, watches, television sets, and a whole host of other mechanical things. Yet product performance inevitably includes an emotional component or meaning, which is where a material good is translated into an experience.

Products perform in many different ways. Fashion brands perform by making the wearer look and feel good. Stylish fashion communicates that one is smart and up-to-date. That kind of emotional performance is equally as valid to the shopper as how well a new dishwasher cleans dishes or how fast a car accelerates.

Retailers must communicate that emotional experience to the shopper and create a context in the store where that meaning is conveyed. It starts with careful product selection, attention-grabbing in-store displays and engaging face-to-face selling. Today specialty retailers need to connect with the shopper by showing how the products "do" (i.e., active verb) something for them, rather than simply "be" a thing (i.e., passive noun).

Rachel Shechtman has made the story or meaning the focus of each new incarnation of STORY. Whether it be a story of Home for the Holidays, Well Being, or Made in America, product selection is based around the theme of the story the store wants to share. Each individual product becomes a chapter in the overall story to be told. Old-fashioned merchandising becomes a new style of curating, carefully selecting each individual product displayed because it presents an essential part of the story being told.

Many specialty retailers depend upon their product brands to offer territorial "exclusivity" in exchange for their business. However, that can put retailers at risk should their reliance on particular product brands conflict with the brand's own plans for growth. While putting specific brands up front in a store's marketing is fine, it is important not to cross the line and let the brands become "the tail that wags the dog." The store must stand on its own, creating its own story and meaning and based upon that story, select brands that communicate the store meaning, not the other way around.

Coventry Corners Evolves to Tell New Stories through New Products with New Meaning

Meet Patricia McLaughlin, who founded Coventry Corners more than 30 years ago, a gift specialty store with two mall locations in southeastern Pennsylvania. Over the years, she has evolved the products and themes for her stores, starting out as a country boutique with a tag line "The Shop That Makes a House a Home." But then things began to change and Pat followed her customers' lead to bring in entirely new ranges of merchandise. In the 1980s and 1990s, she expanded the store from its home décor focus into collectibles, transforming the Coventry Corners brand as a result. "We became the area's premier dealer in collectibles with over 20,000 collectors in our clubs and ranked second in the state for selling Yankee Candles," she said.

But that was then, this is now. Today Coventry Corners has ventured far afield of country "tchotchkes" and collectible knickknacks. Pat explains, "You have to keep going in a new direction. When you see something slowing down or you see it everywhere, then it is time for a change." Part of that change meant swapping out product lines, even high-performing brands like Yankee Candle that contributed to the stores' original growth and success. Today Coventry doesn't carry Yankee Candles because so many other stores sell them. "They tried to be everything for everybody. It's everywhere," Pat says.

The key for Pat in finding a new direction for the store was two-fold: to not only listen to what the customers want, but to then go out and find it. "The people we listen to are our customers. They ask for things that nobody else has, like this kind of belt, so we go out and find those belts. What makes us stand out—our main thing which is ingrained in our staff—is paying attention to detail in every aspect of everything we do. From what the staff wears, what we buy, it is all a big package."

That "big package" is the Coventry Corners' brand itself. And today, taking the lead from its customers, the store has been reimagined from a country home décor and collectible store into a fashion boutique. Pat now tells a "Decorate Yourself" story, selling jewelry, fashion accessories and other specialty wearable items. The store is merchandised around the brands it sells, with each brand showcased to tell its unique brand story. The premiere brands include Vera Bradley bags, Uggs, ALEX AND ANI, PANDORA, Brighton, and Marianna Crystals, but her stores' branding doesn't depend upon these brands; rather she and her staff select the product brands that support the story that she wants to share with her customers.

Regarding new product selection, Pat brings a long-term perspective spanning three decades in specialty retail. "Good things only last 7 or 8 years, then they go away, but then sometimes, they come back," she says. For example, in the early 1990s Coventry Corners was an early adopter of the Vera Bradley fashion accessories line, but the timing just wasn't right. "We carried it for 2 years, but it did not sell, so we sold it off at our sidewalk sale. Then in 1999, I noticed how it was having a resurgence and I started to see it on more people. So we got it back again. In 2010 we were the third largest independent dealer of Vera Bradley in the country and I am on their advisory board."

Looking to the future, Pat is starting to hand over the day-to-day operations of the store to her daughter, Megan, who brings a degree in marketing to the business, along with professional experience outside of retail. Pat brags, "She is that good and better than I ever was." With Megan taking the lead, Coventry Corners is poised to continue its evolution, guided by the wishes and desires of its next generation customers.

Beauty, and Quality, Are in the Eyes of the Beholder

Whenever you talk with customers about why they select one item over another, quality always ranks as critically important in their choice. Buying decisions invariably hinge on people's perception of better quality. But as the Cornell Food Lab teaches us, the perception of quality is powerfully influenced by the context in which the item is measured. While customers tend to view quality as quantitative and objectively measurable, quality is very much subjective and can be influenced. That calls on retailers to research the many different dimensions of quality that characterize their product categories and how the shopper ultimately perceives them.

There is an interconnection between an individual store and the quality and brands of the products they choose to carry. The quality of the products reflects back on how shoppers perceive the quality of the store, as do the store's brand and merchandising selections. For example, Pat McLaughlin defines the strategy she uses for Coventry Corners in selecting new fashion brands. She looks for brands that she calls "Fabulously Funky." She explains, "I try hard to get items $30 and under that make a fashion statement, like a necklace and earring set. In jewelry we try to find elegant-looking costume jewelry at a reasonable price so everybody can get that 'designer look.' ALEX AND ANI fits into that mold. It's that perfect price point, $28, and something that everyone can wear. It makes a great gift from teacher to grandmother."

The Product Must Touch the Shopper's Hot Buttons

The importance of product for a specialty retailer boils down to how much the product touches specific personal hot buttons for the shopper. People don't buy an item simply because it is good quality, made by this or that designer, or any other specific feature. They buy the product for the specific performance attributes it promises to deliver, whether those attributes are mechanical or emotional. The value inherent in quality is meaningful when translated into the way quality improves performance, i.e., the way the thing performs for the consumer and how it does what it is supposed to do. Quality has to be looked at from the customers' perspective.

The key is translating the specific quality measures that the product possesses. In the case of Coventry Corners, for example, rather than just buying a ALEX AND ANI charm bracelet for $28, the customer is really buying something that makes her feel "fabulous" and "funky." In other words, through the careful curation of its brands and the product features that the brands offer, Coventry Corners becomes a destination where one can find fabulous and funky things for oneself or to give as a gift, all at an affordable price.

Chapter 5

Affordability

Both Absolute and Relative Affordability

"I don't own any of my own paintings because a Picasso original costs several thousand dollars – it's a luxury I can't afford."

—Pablo Picasso

When talking to specialty retailers, one thing heard over and over again is price – their customers are incredibly price sensitive and they can't compete with the big box retailers that can sell it cheaper. But as in all things marketing, the customers' perception is reality. As *Mad Men*'s Don Draper famously said, "If you don't like what's being said, change the conversation." Our opportunity is to change the conversation around price to what it really is for the customer: affordability. And we believe the way customers interpret price has two different perspectives: Absolute affordability, i.e., can the customer afford to buy it, and relative affordability, i.e., is the customer willing to pay for it? These are two entirely different questions.

Absolute affordability is simply a measure of whether one's budget or bank account can stretch to meet the purchase. On the other hand, most buying decisions rest on relative affordability, or how much a particular purchase is worth to the individual shopper.

We all understand the concept of absolute affordability and virtually 99.9 percent of all Americans live under some constraints of absolute affordability – for example, whether or not one can swing the payments for a personal jet and its monthly upkeep, or the monthly time-share fee for the "virtual" ownership of a personal jet, or simply the cost of a round trip ticket on Jet Blue from New York to Los Angeles. The concept of absolute affordability is clear.

Where things become hazy is in the realm of relative affordability – how much is that purchase worth to the customer? How much money is the shopper willing to trade off to make that purchase? For example, is he or she willing to cut back on the enjoyment of daily double lattes and brown bag lunch to work every day for the next month in order to pay for a week's Caribbean cruise?

To Encourage Buying, National Retailers Push the Affordability Button Hardest

In examining the key attributes that influence the shopper's propensity to buy – Need, Features, and Affordability – the affordability hot button is the one that mass and big-box retailers and marketers push most aggressively and most consistently in order to stimulate shoppers to make purchases. It's called sales and discounts.

As we have seen, retailers and marketers are largely powerless in the realm of need. They can't make anyone need their products, though they have the ability to make their product desired. They can pump up the product features to make an item highly desirable and better than all the rest, but in most instances, people don't buy an item in the store simply because of its features. They need more than that; they need the potential purchase to touch their emotional hot buttons, and this is where affordability comes into play, making the perceived value of the item for sale worth the value that it promises to deliver to the customer.

Every retailer faces this challenge and specialty retailers more so. Depending upon the price, an item can be transformed from something the shopper simply overlooks into an item to die for and that has to be bought immediately.

A recent Unity Marketing survey among shoppers found that nearly two-thirds agreed with the statement, "I often buy things I see on sale that I don't strictly need, but are at such a good price that I can't pass them up." For many specialty retailers with less pricing flexibility than big boxes, it is the price, and often times the price alone, that moves the shopper to buy.

Specialty Retailers Must Focus on Special Customers: the Affluent

Having come through the Great Recession, the reputed sharpest decline in the U.S. economy since the Depression of the 1930s, and which officially lasted from December 2007 to June 2009, the average American household income dropped by 4 percent in 2013 dollars. The decline was even more pronounced since 2000 – a 6 percent reduction in the average American household's income from $77,287 in 2000 to $72,641 in 2013.

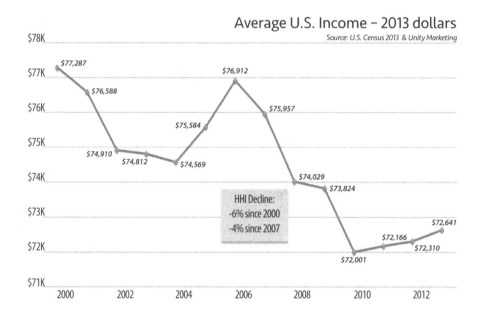

Average U.S. Income – 2013 dollars
Source: U.S. Census 2013 & Unity Marketing

The causes of this income decline are numerous, but needless to say the average American household lost $4,646 in spending power in the 21st century and over the short term they don't look like they will recover that loss, let alone grow their incomes and spending power, over the next decade or so.

These are the harsh economic realities the average American consumer faces. But amid the economic doom and gloom there is one hope for specialty retailers: the affluent consumer segment at the top 20 percent of household incomes. These are the customers that specialty retailers need to focus on, to lure them into their shops and encourage them to buy.

While even the affluent top 20 percent has seen their incomes drop since 2000, the decline has not been as sharp as the average U.S. household, only about 4 percent, and because their average income is more than 2.5 times greater than the average household, they have significantly greater spending power. The approximately 28 million households at the top 20 percent are the customer segment that specialty retailers need to aim for.

Often when the word "affluent" is mentioned, people get confused and imagine the picture of affluence that the media portrays, like CNBC's *Secret Lives of the Super Rich,* or the *Wall Street Journal Magazine,* billed as the world's leading luxury magazine. But the vast majority of affluents, some 24 million or 90 percent of those at the top 20 percent, are the mass-affluent HENRYs – high earners not rich yet – with incomes from about $100K to $249.9K. The HENRYs view themselves as decidedly middle-class. While their high levels of income relative to the average household allows them to occasionally trade up to luxury, on a day-to-day basis they typically live a fairly modest lifestyle. Yet it is ultimately their greater discretionary spending power that specialty retailers must attract by delivering the kind of over-the-top product and services experiences that they will appreciate at prices that seem modest in comparison.

Doyle & Doyle –
Presenting Luxurious, yet Affordable Jewelry
to a Special Kind of Customer

New York City-based jeweler Doyle & Doyle succeeds by focusing on a special kind of customer that truly appreciates the unique kind of jewelry product and shopping experience that it offers: vintage, antique, and estate jewelry. Doyle & Doyle was founded in 2000 by sisters, Elizabeth and Pamela Doyle, and recently relocated to West 13th Street in New York City's Meatpacking District.

Unlike so many Madison and Fifth Avenue jewelry stores that sell jewelry to the uptown crowd, Doyle & Doyle is a jewelry store with a downtown difference. "We specifically opened downtown because we are 'downtown' girls. We saw this void in the market. We wanted to bring vintage and estate jewelry downtown in a very accessible way, both in price point and location, and by being open and welcoming to our customer. Even though we were selling the same merchandise as uptown, we differentiated ourselves right away by being downtown. The difference starts from the moment you enter the store," Elizabeth said.

While the price for rare antique jewelry can easily range into 5 or 6 figures, Doyle & Doyle set out to sell "pretty things, everyday jewelry that didn't break the bank, but that was interesting." The target customers were not the uptown "ladies who lunch," though they'd be welcome there too, but the creative-class young people who live and work downtown. Elizabeth explained, "Uptown, generally, you find customers with more money, who are more established and older, but the younger, more creative types are drawn downtown. They feel more comfortable here, working and going out. There is a lot of creative industry here too, publishing, graphics, technology. Established stores uptown have been selling the same antique jewelry for a long time to a more affluent, older customer. Our customer is interested in vintage with a cool, creative style and we found a huge market for it."

Being experts on both vintage jewelry and what their customers want, Doyle & Doyle helps them find that special piece of jewelry that will truly become their own, whether the customer has a starving-artist budget or that of a Wall Street financier. Elizabeth said, "We have a huge price range here, anything from under $200 up to $50,000-$60,000-$100,000. We have customers who have different spending power, but it doesn't mean they can't be comfortable here. We provide an experience where people feel they are getting something really good for whatever they are spending. We have people who come in and don't have a lot to spend, but when they leave, they feel it is so special. No matter what somebody spends, it is a lot to them, it is luxurious to them."

In the world of vintage jewelry, people love to hunt for that special piece; it is an important part of the whole shopping experience. The Doyle & Doyle sales team is trained to help customers find their special treasure. "We are not here to sell, we are here to help you find what you need. That is what people appreciate, that is why they come back to us. We are not trying to sell them, we are not trying to push the price up or make the sale. We are really focused on what they want and getting them what they need," Elizabeth explained.

Finding that one-of-a-kind piece for special customers at a price they can afford has led the store to specialize in one of the most important emotional experience in anyone's life: bridal and wedding. "When we opened, we thought we were going to sell low-priced, pretty, everyday wearable vintage jewelry, but early on people came in looking for engagement rings and that is predominately our business now. But it wasn't our plan," Elizabeth said.

The engagement ring customer is drawn to the one-of-a-kind nature of vintage. A Doyle & Doyle ring isn't going to be like any-one else's. Elizabeth says, "You know when that ring is your ring. When she puts it on her finger, it comes to life and it doesn't do that for everyone. It breathes life into the ring, and life into the person. It is a magical moment. Once it is theirs, it is theirs and no one else's."

For Doyle & Doyle selling jewelry is ultimately not about the jewelry item itself, but about filling the customer's deeply personal need with a special piece of jewelry that symbolizes the emotional connection, at a price he or she can afford. Elizabeth said, "People need an engagement ring. It is a very important symbol. It is not just buying a ring, but going through the whole process. Today most couples go through that process together. In picking out the engagement ring, they work out all kinds of things that are important in embarking on a life together. They talk about budgets, what is important to them, style, aesthetic, price. They make compromises, until they get to a place they both feel good about. That is when they know they can be engaged and now they are ready to move on to being married."

In meeting their customers' needs, Doyle & Doyle recently intro-duced its own Heirloom collection with historically-inspired designs, but with the brand's distinctive "downtown" style. Elizabeth explains the Heirloom collection fills voids in estate jewelry, like stud ear-rings, that people ask for, but simply can't be found in vintage.

"Now we do full collections on a theme. It's been a fun addition to our business," she says.

Doyle & Doyle's business is to match the customers' aesthetics with their budgets to find that special something that becomes truly "their own." They have a vast range of antique and vintage jewelry, combined with their exclusive Heirloom collection to do just that. "We get as much, if not more satisfaction, out of struggling to find that piece that is special and affordable than selling a big piece. That is because it is so important to those people, even more so when they are on a tight budget. They appreciate it so much. Those customers are as valuable to us as the ones that spend more money," Elizabeth concludes.

Specialty Retailers Don't Compete on Price, They Compete on Value

"We can afford all that we need; but we cannot afford all that we want." —Franklin D. Roosevelt

Even in the world of the affluent consumers, discount prices are a big draw. People who can afford to pay full price simply don't have to. They know where to find the discounts and take advantage of them freely when shopping. Those with affluent levels of income can pay more and are willing to pay more when the value (i.e., the meaning) is really there. Too often, however, they opt for paying less, because they can easily find whatever they want for less. Specialty retailers need to focus on what makes their stores, their products, their overall experiences special and thus command a higher price.

Specialty retailers, rather than becoming part of the over-stored, over-merchandised problem, must become part of the solution. Specialty retailers must narrow down the selection for their customers and carefully curate the range of products that meet their special customers' needs at prices they are willing to pay. They must refuse to be all things to all people, the kiss of death in specialty retail. Just ask Patricia McLaughlin of Coventry Corners about Yankee Candle.

As a specialty retailer you need to narrow cast your business to attract the highest-value customers, the affluent living in your community for whom absolute affordability won't be a deal breaker, with products and shopping experiences that they truly value and are willing to pay for. So you have to attract the right customers ultimately by satisfying the customers' emotional experiences. Elizabeth Doyle understands this and makes that the heart of the Doyle & Doyle jewelry experience, "In an easy world where anything is available, finding that special something is what it is all about. It is the process of going through it. For some, the harder it is, the more meaningful it is. That makes it personal."

Chapter 6

Emotions

The Key to Driving Sales Is to Push Shoppers' Emotional Hot Buttons

Carrie: *Hon, if it hurts so much, why are we going shopping?*

Samantha: *I have a broken toe, not a broken spirit.*

—Sex and the City

As much as we would like objective, quantifiable criteria, such as product features and price, to drive shoppers to make purchases, ultimately shoppers' emotions play the dominant and most pivotal role. Emotions transform need into desire. Emotions color the way the shopper interprets specific product features. Emotions turn a shopper from one who can afford to make a purchase into someone willing to do so. Emotions play off and magnify all the other factors – need, features, affordability – to make the item irresistible. A retail store is more than just a cash register and a bunch of merchandise displayed on shelves. It represents a shopping experience for the customer that is infinitely more than just going to a store and buying stuff.

! A retail store represents a shopping experience for the customer that is infinitely more than just buying stuff.

As we have seen, shoppers' needs in and of themselves are only a small part of the reason why people buy. Rather it is the impact of emotion and how shoppers interpret their emotional desires as real and compelling needs that ultimately tips the scale toward buy. As we scan across the consumer landscape, there is one place we find a segment where true need plays virtually no role in the shopping formula and that is in the $70 billion American luxury market.

Luxury Is in the Eye of the Beholder

There are lots of definitions about what "luxury" is today. The word luxury comes with so much baggage that the image it conjures in people's minds may bear little or no resemblance to a clear and concise marketplace definition that those who study the consumer market need. Is it brand? Is it price point? Is it some combination of quality, style, design, and workmanship?

Ultimately luxury is a mindset, not a price point or brand. Consumers define luxury for themselves personally, according to their own internal needs and drives. What one person considers a luxury may be very different from what another does, and who can argue that each of the unique, personal, subjective definitions of luxury is wrong? The customer is the final arbiter of what luxury is, not some external authority like a designer, company marketer, advertiser, or anybody else.

However, there seems to be one overriding way to look at luxury and that is "more more," as a consumer described it in an interview. Luxury is "more more," meaning it is more than anyone needs, over the top more, the pinnacle more, the ultimate more, the extraordinary more. So depending upon one's particular vantage point, the consensus definition, the one that best fits today's world of luxury, is that luxury is more than what anyone really needs.

Therefore, we all might need a pair of jeans and we can buy a good quality, long lasting, nationally recognized brand in the $50 to $60 range and under. Nobody needs to pay $200 to $300 for a pair of jeans. Anyone can find perfectly good substitutes for far less, so who can argue that a pair of $200 7 For All Mankind distressed jeans, with holes carefully crafted, is anything but a luxury.

The luxury market ultimately is one driven solely and totally by desire, not need. Savvy retailers at all levels in the retailing sphere, from Walmart and Target, JC Penney, and Gap, are taking a lead from the luxury marketers and retailers in order to move from their more or less needs-based retailing model into one driven by desire. Satisfying

! While nobody needs luxury, everybody wants it!

shopper desires, not their needs, is where the serious money is to be made. It is tapping into the emotion behind all consumer purchases, from the most mundane to the most extraordinary, and appealing to shoppers' emotional desires, not the normal, physical, everyday needs. While nobody needs luxury, everybody wants it!

Specialty retailing is all about discretion: selling discretionary products bought at the discretion of the shopper with their discretionary income. Discretion is key, and luxury is at the top of the discretionary pyramid. Thus nobody needs luxury, but everybody at some level wants the pleasure of it. It brings self-fulfillment and satisfies deep-seated personal desires, with the result that it brings personal transformation and is a means toward self-actualization, in Dr. Maslow's terms.

Our culture is fascinated by the concept of self-actualization and personal transformation. The reality television craze, including shows like *Survivor, Love It or List It, American Idol, Dancing with the Stars, Biggest Loser, Say Yes to the Dress,* and all the rest, reflect this passionate interest to watch and vicariously participate in personal transformation.

While all these shows focus on transformation on the outside, (i.e., a newly designed house, a new body, new style, new talent), in actuality the real transformation is taking place on the inside with the participants stretching themselves, challenging their old assumptions about themselves, trying on new identities, and learning new skills. By watching these shows, viewers are reassured about trying out their own personal transformation in order to test how far they can fulfill a newly idealized personal identity.

And this then, the need to fulfill one's self-actualization needs, is what shoppers truly are in search of. Everyone wants it and everyone needs it: to craft a more idealized, self-actualized version of his or her self. Buying things helps them do that.

For example, some customers shop for the latest fashion to self-actualize by projecting an external image that conforms to their internal image. Some shoppers self-actualize through their homes, so how their homes are decorated, cleaned, organized, and presented to the world, are their canvases for personal transformation; their spending focuses on home-related things. Others self-actualize through their children, so a mother may shop for her own clothes at T.J.Maxx or Kohl's, but spare no expense for fashion for her kids. Many men self-actualize through technology or technical accomplishments, thus they buy new computers or new

> ❗ Material goods can help achieve self-actualization and transformation, but true, lasting, profound changes come through experiences.

tools to help them self-actualize through these mediums. Further, most people have several areas in which they self-actualize, so they make purchases in many different categories to fulfill different self-actualization needs. While material goods can help one achieve self-actualization and transformation, the lasting, most profound changes come through experiences.

Psychologists Leaf Van Boven and Thomas Gilovich conducted a study about consumer happiness and satisfaction and published the findings in the *Journal of Personality and Psychology* (vol. 85, no. 6, 2003). The study was called "To Do or to Have? That is the question." In their research they never used the word "luxury." They studied consumers across all income levels, not just the affluent, and they found basically the same thing. They found consumers' greatest source of happiness did not derive from the material goods they bought, but from their acquisition of "life experiences." They write, "'The good life,' in other words, may be better lived by *doing* things than by *having* things."

These findings about the shift to experiences give a clear wake-up call to retailers and marketers everywhere. The goods they create and sell simply are not enough anymore for shoppers. They desire more fulfillment, more happiness, more personal transformation, and more self-actualization than material goods can ever provide.

That is why at its most basic level, retailers must embrace an entirely new business model that focuses on the shopping experience, not the things or merchandise that they sell. And the next generation of customers, the Millennials, may well be more driven toward self-actualization at a younger age, because as a generation they have grown up in a digital, connected, virtual world of cell phones, internet, and social media. Living in a virtual world as they do, they use these media as the tools for self-actualization, so it is likely that such needs for self-actualization will propel them as consumers and shoppers as they mature.

Retailers Can Play off a Whole Host of Other Emotional Factors to Encourage Shoppers to Spend More

With their overriding emphasis on product and price, retailers often overlook the many varied dimensions of the shopping experience that they could use to play to the shoppers' emotions. While sales and discounts draw people into stores, offering up a really special shopping environment every day, like shops that POP! do, is a powerful strategy to attract people to shop.

What shoppers are looking for from the people in the store is to feel special. Women, in particular, are the caregivers in the family and they tend to put their husbands, children, and everybody else first. So when they are shopping – out getting their retail therapy – they want someone to cater to their needs and desires.

A shopper said in a discussion group, "Service is service. They need to put service back into the experience. I am not going so far as to say the customer is always right, but they have to give you the service and put your needs first."

Putting Service Back into the Shopping Experience

While the retail industry is moving more into the self-service realm with stores located in destination shopping malls, shoppers feel nostalgic for the old days when shopping was an event you got dressed up for and went downtown for a full day of browsing, shopping, and experiencing. This Atlanta shopper longs for when you went downtown to shop. "I like more of the downtown-shopping atmosphere because you also have cafés and places where you can sit outdoors. It's more fun to people watch while they're shopping – it is just more for recreation. It is more European style where you can shop and eat and be with friends. I think it's sad that downtown shopping is gone."

Part of what is missing under the new self-service mall-based retailing paradigm is knowledgeable salespeople who really know their stuff. In Unity Marketing's discussions with shoppers they talk about how nice it is to go into a store and have someone wait on them who knows the products, knows what they carry, and can advise on what is the best item to buy. Too many retailers today staff their stores with minimum-wage, part-time workers assigned to housewares one day and the jewelry counter the next. No wonder, when shoppers ask questions, they get blank stares.

One person who knows all about crafting the shopper's emotional experiences is Mary Liz Curtin. She has worked on both sides

of specialty retail business, as a consultant and adviser to marketers that provide products to those businesses, and as a specialty
independent shop keeper. Mary Liz is a writer, including being the
author of *A Shopkeeper's Manual – A practical workbook for the
independent retailer: Be a Better Merchant, Raise Your Margins,
Lower Your Costs, Make More Money, Have More Fun,* a contributing columnist to *The Wall Street Journal*'s Small Business experts'
blog, and an invited speaker to a whole host of trade shows and
industry events focused on specialty retailing.

But first and foremost Mary Liz, along with her husband, operate
Leon & Lulu, a lifestyle store focused on home furnishings, gifts and
accessories located in Clawson, Michigan, a Detroit suburb. Their
store is in a local landmark building, the Ambassador Skating Rink,
built in 1941. Leon & Lulu was named on *Home Accent Today*'s list
of the nation's 50 "retail stars" for 2015.

The couple's overwhelming retail success led to the recent acquisition of a neighboring historic space, Clawson Theatre, which will
add nearly 8,000 square feet of entertaining retail space once the
renovation of the movie theater is complete. No doubt, Mary Liz
will preserve the retail as theater experience in the new space, as
she does currently in the Leon & Lulu store where greeters work in
roller skates. That sets the tone of fun and frolic in the store and
creates an unforgettable customer experience from the very start.

Leon & Lulu Becomes Part of the Shoppers' Celebration

Forging an emotional connection with the customer is critical to
success as a small- to mid-size retailer, but it's one that too many
business owners don't think much about. "People don't even recognize the emotional connection," says Mary Liz. But this is a tragic
error, because a retailer can be a partner in many emotional events
that stay with customers long after they leave the store.

"For a big event, like a wedding or a birthday, part of the
celebration is shopping," says Mary Liz. Selecting a gift, an outfit,
or just the right caterer or venue becomes part of the emotional
fabric of the milestone, and the right retailer will become a friend
to the event host or guest. Such connections are priceless in today's
retailing environment, where good word of mouth translates into

money in the bank down the line. Transcending the role of shop owner and becoming a friend is the key part of the emotional experience. "People like to shop with their friends; it doesn't matter if you're a gas station or a full-service boutique like us," says Mary Liz.

Leon & Lulu offers an eclectic blend of furniture, clothing, accessories, and gifts in its unique retail environment. There, Curtin and her staff provide the kind of experience that brings customers in to interact with both staff and merchandise. "People like to pick things up, get fingerprints on it, and put it back in the wrong place," she says with good humor.

Offering a unique selection of products across a wide range of customer experiences, from kitchen to bath, to living room as well as fashion and accessories for the closet, is key to the store's shopper appeal. She says, "Lately I have learned that I am a curator, with a carefully edited collection. We proudly exhibit a selection of artisanal products, from small batch vendors, global resources or crowd-sourced makers."

Shoppers' desire for interaction is part of what is driving retailers who originally envisioned themselves as "online only" to open bricks-and-mortar stores in order to be successful. "People like immediate gratification," Curtin says, noting that only in person can a customer try on an outfit and take it home the same hour.

Additionally, this gives the store staff a chance to form a bond with the customer and be sure she makes a selection that will make her happy. For clothing, it's important to have knowledgeable staff standing by to advise on fit, trends, accompanying pieces, and accessories.

Furniture is another such area. Curtin tells of one customer who wanted to purchase a fabric ottoman even though she had three small boys and a love of red wine. She counseled the customer into buying a coffee table instead, as the hard surface would be more conducive to life with children who could knock over glasses of wine.

Curtin has also tied Leon & Lulu's success to offering a wide variety of merchandise. She notes how difficult it was to sell furniture in 2008 when the Great Recession hit. "We were lucky to have small things to balance the sales." But today, those customers who bought the small indulgences and gifts in 2008 are back to buy big-ticket furniture.

Leon & Lulu stays nimble by having a wide diversity of offerings. "Our store is a complete destination, so we're overstocked at all times," she says. She encourages others to do the same. "If business is bad, that's not the time to stop stocking. When people come in, they need to see things have changed." And even if it's not practical to add new stock at the same rate, the existing stock needs to continually move into new configurations, "no matter how many times you've moved that same frog," she says.

Understand What You Are Really Selling – Customer Experiences

Mary Liz understands that what she is selling (the products that fill the Leon & Lulu store) is not what the customer is ultimately buying (emotionally compelling shopping experiences). She notes that all the really great brands understand this too, from FedEx, which is selling package delivery but its customers are buying dependability, or Starbucks, which sells coffee while its customers are buying that "third place" between work and home where they can meet and create a community, to Apple which sells technology, but customers are buying fashion and design.

The key is to focus on the customer experience that is delivered by the products you sell, store environment and service delivery. Mary Liz counsels, "Your customer base is the most important asset you have. When a bigger business moves into your space, it is even more important to understand your clientele, know who they are and what they need from you. While we 'indies' cannot compete on price, the relationships we build with our customers, the service we offer, and the careful selection of offerings keeps us in business. Whatever the size of your business, always think of your customers first. Make their experience with your business as fabulous as it can be and they will not want to leave."

And that, my friends, is the secret recipe for specialty retail success. Now let's turn to the experiences that you can create in your store to transform it from a place that sells stuff into a true customer experience – a shop that POPs!

PART 2

Retailing Stars

Secret Sauce that Turns
an Ordinary Store into
a Shop that POPS!

Chapter 7

The POP! Equation –
Your Recipe for Retailing Success

"Whoever said money can't buy happiness simply didn't know where to go shopping."

—Bo Derek

With an understanding of the customers, what motivates them and what drives them to the store and gets them to buy, now we turn our attention to the secret sauce that transforms an ordinary, run-of-the-mill store into a shop that POPs! by creating extraordinary experiences for the customer. The POP! Equation defines the unique way that retailers apply specific strategies and combine them to create a truly special, extraordinary shopping experience for the customer.

> ❗ The POP! Equation defines the unique way that retailers apply specific strategies and combine them to create a truly special, extraordinary shopping experience for the customer.

Academic researchers and environmental psychologists Robert Donovan and John Rossiter conducted a seminal study of how a store's atmosphere impacts customers' shopping behavior. Published in the *Journal of Retailing* in 1994 (vol. 70, issue 3) "Store Atmosphere and Purchasing Behavior" found a direct and causal link between shopper emotions and how they spend in the store. They write: "The practical significance for retailers is that emotional responses induced by the store environment can affect the time and money that consumers spend in the store."

Very simply put, shoppers will spend more time in a store that is a pleasant, engaging, and happy place to be. Their happiness and delight will result in them spending more money, which will translate into greater success for the retailer who makes that happen. And this is exactly what the POP! Equation is about – a seven-point recipe that special retailers can use to transform their stores into a place that shoppers want to spend more time and thus spend money.

Shops that POP!, like pet boutique Godfrey's, gift store and restaurant Grapevine Farms, New York City's magazine-cum-gallery-cum-retail store STORY, home furnishings boutique Nell Hill's, grocer Dorothy Lane Market, gifts and fashion boutique Coventry Corners, jewelry store Doyle & Doyle, and lifestyle boutique Leon & Lulu, exhibit each of these qualities to a greater or lesser extent. You can follow this guide to make your special store POP! too.

Here is the seven-point recipe to make a shop POP!

Customer involvement and interaction. Shops that POP! create a shopping environment that fully involves the shopper and engages them interactively in the shopping experience. Shoppers don't just browse the aisles and participate as passive observers. Shops that POP! encourage customers to touch, feel, taste, try on, and participate in the store in a more involving way. Think of the difference between a store that posts signs "You broke it – You bought it!" as compared with a store that invites you to touch, feel, and explore, like Grapevine Farms, where shoppers are invited to enjoy the aroma and taste of homemade cookies. Those cookies are a tempting way to welcome customers to the homelike, comforting experience of the store.

Evokes shopper curiosity. Shops that POP! excite consumer curiosity to explore and experience from the shop windows and entrance through the different displays. They lure shoppers into the store and then to turn the next corner and walk down the next aisle to find that wonderful treasures are just out of sight. Curiosity about what treasures they may find causes customers to spend hours just getting to, not to mention shopping in, Nell Hill's. They want to make sure they don't miss anything exciting.

Contagious, electric quality. Shops that POP! exude energy and excitement that is contagious. Think about how much electricity and excitement is conveyed by Leon & Lulu's greeters on roller skates. Shoppers catch it and return again and again to the store to rev up their engines. The contagion also spreads through word of mouth to make the shop a destination for people in the community, the state, even across the country. It is this quality that makes a shop that POPs! a happening place, exciting to visit, and a thrill to participate in. Even shoppers who are not all that into the category feel there is something in the store for them. Godfrey's makes the customer experience electric with the many things for their pets to see and do there, as well as the irresistible fun of being greeted at the door by Godfrey's four-legged ambassador.

Convergence between atmosphere, store design, and merchandise. Shops that POP! present a comprehensive vision that captures all the tangible and intangible elements of the store in a unified whole. This quality of convergence extends far beyond a cookie-cutter, homogenized, neutralized shopping environment. These shops present distinctive points of view that tie together all the disparate elements of the store into one experience. Leon & Lulu expertly ties together its funky location, in an old skating rink, with funky merchandise that showcases the new, different, and trendy for home and for oneself.

Expresses an authentic concept. Shops that POP! are more than stores selling stuff; they are conceptually driven and reflect a visionary's values. A shop that POPs! transcends being just a store into a new realm of experience. Doyle & Doyle evokes such authenticity selling antique and vintage jewelry as well as jewelry designed by its founders, sisters Elizabeth and Pamela Doyle. Doyle & Doyle is an authentic expression of the sisters' personalities and charm. That is what draws customers in, as much as the wonderful jewelry.

Priced right for the value. Shops that POP! have a carefully constructed pricing strategy based upon offering fair value delivered to the shopper for a reasonable price. That is, they try to maximize the value of the goods offered and price them right. Pricing is not about how low you can go, but about how much value can you offer at a good and fair price to the shopper. Pricing, therefore, hinges upon the value for the shopper, not necessarily the money. Dorothy Lane Market is not the least expensive grocery store in Dayton, Ohio, but it is one that delivers carefully selected food products in a setting designed specifically to meet the needs of busy 21st century food shoppers. Yet it still offers the nostalgic old-time neighborhood grocery store feel from the mid-20th century when DLM was founded.

Accessible, nonexclusive, and free from pretensions. Shops that POP! have all the preceding qualities, plus another essential feature – they are immediately accessible to everyone, free from pretensions of exclusivity or snobbishness. They know they are good, but rather than resting on their laurels and expecting everybody else to know it too, they are constantly reaching out, drawing people into their web with missionary zeal and self-effacing charm. It is all about making the shopper feel personally welcome, as Coventry Corners does in its mall stores, where the contrast between the inviting and friendly Coventry Corners' staff and the national chain fashion boutique next door staffed with indifferent, overworked and largely untrained sales clerks are so sharply contrasted.

What's Next

The Shops that POP! we have looked at all get the formula right. They deliver engaging shopping experiences to their customers that stimulate their curiosity, make them feel welcome, invite them to explore, and most importantly, encourage them to buy. In other words, they love their customers and make shopping there fun, which is absolutely contagious to the customers and in turn makes the customer love shopping there.

In the chapters that follow we explore in more detail each of the qualities that make up the POP! Equation through case studies of retailers that are doing it right. We draw upon in-depth interviews conducted with independent retailers to understand how they work the magic in their store and what makes them POP! for the shopper.

Chapter 8

Create the Ultimate Customer Experience

Create Opportunities for Customer Involvement and Interaction

"When the customer comes first, the customer will last."

—Robert Half

Having looked at the challenges of retailing today and explored the shoppers' experiences, now we turn our attention to specific steps retailers can take to make theirs a shop that POPs! The strategy is simple: Love your customers by making shopping in your store truly a special experience. The focus for retailing success in the future is not so much what you sell, but how you sell it. The focus for retailing success in the future is not so much what you sell, but how you sell it.

> ❗ The focus for retailing success in the future is not so much what you sell, but how you sell it.

Retailers, especially the small independent types who offer a limited range of merchandise in a limited space with a limited operating budget, recognize that their special shopping experience doesn't appeal to everybody. That is the role of mass retailers: to sell to the masses.

What specialty retailers must focus on is the type of shopper that responds best to their unique combination of products and services. And that is largely the shopper looking for something new and different, in search of pleasure and fun, as much as looking for products to buy. So the competitive secret for small specialty stores is to make shopping in their store special and fun.

POP! Factor #1

Maximize Customer Involvement by Appealing to All the Senses

Grapevine Farms engages its customers in a multisensory way. It offers the latest designs from leading fashion brands, along with decorative accents for the home, in a welcoming environment made even more homelike by the aroma of cookies baking.

Shoppers come into one store with the potential to engage all five senses – sight, sound, touch, taste, and smell. Too many stores play to only one or two of the potential points of involvement. The more sensory touch points a retailer can engage the customer in, the better their chances of building a true community with the customer. The more sensory touch points a retailer can engage the customer in, the better their chances of building a true community with the customer.

> ! The more sensory touch points a retailer can engage the customer in, the better their chances of building a true community with the customer.

When a store builds community with its customers, it isn't long before the customers themselves begin to build a community among themselves and that is when real magic happens. People have a tremendous need today to connect with other people. Many of us derive our sense of community from our extended families, the workplace, our neighborhoods, and churches, but it is harder and harder to feel truly connected with others today as we spread out into the suburbs and live narrowly prescribed, overscheduled lives.

Godfrey's excels at providing a sense of community to both its four-legged customers and their two-legged parents. While the commercial nature of the relationship greases the wheels, Godfrey's creates an environment in which meaningful connections are made and where Barb Emmett and her staff honestly have customers' interests, both two-and-four-legged, in mind.

Nell Hill's Mary Carol Garrity has made creating an atmosphere that maximizes customer involvement a cornerstone of her marketing plan. How else does one explain that she has built a very successful business based upon attracting shoppers who live over an hour away? Mary Carol sets the tone by spending 100 percent of her time in the store on the sales floor rubbing elbows and chatting with the customers. Because Nell Hill's is a destination store in the true sense of the word, people who visit are not casual, but very committed, having invested so much travel time just to get there. Because of that, they want to share their excitement with Mary Carol, her staff, and other shoppers in the store.

Shoppers come to Nell Hill's for the wonderful, innovative home furnishings offered, but they are equally drawn by the charged atmosphere, the warm welcome they get from the proprietor, and the chance to establish a sense of community with other shoppers in the store. Mary Carol says shopping in her store is like a cocktail party without the alcohol. She carries that high level of customer involvement even into her personal life. She has opened her home up to her customers through regular open houses when they can tour her home and stop off by the tent out back and buy interesting items that aren't even featured in the store. Another hallmark of Mary Carol's customer involvement is doing special events outside the four walls of the store.

By reaching out into the community and going to them, not waiting for them to come to her store, Mary Carol has attracted a passionate crowd of shoppers, near and far, who regularly visit her store to find out what's new, both in terms of merchandise and in Mary Carol's life as well.

Feast! –
Feed Them and They Will Come

In a corner of a market hall of independent food shops in Charlottesville, Virginia, home of Thomas Jefferson and the University of Virginia, is an artisan cheese and gourmet store called Feast! You have got to go out of your way to find it, but when you do it is an absolute delight for all your senses, but most especially the taste buds, because everywhere you turn there are sample bowls to tempt you to try all the wonderful foods on display.

Recognized as one of the top 20 cheese shops in America by *Saveur* magazine and named by the Specialty Food Association as one of its five winners of the 2013 Outstanding Retailer Awards, Feast!'s founder, Kate Collier, and her husband, Eric Gertner, operate their store based upon a simple principle: "If someone asks about something, rather than tell them what it tastes like, we put it in their mouths."

❗ "If people ask about something, rather than tell them what it tastes like, we put it in their mouths."

Food is so basic and sharing food such an important way to build community that Feast! takes advantage of that at every turn in the store. Kate explains, "One of our employees has been with us since we opened and he knows everybody's name and what they eat. So when they walk in, he says, 'Hi, Mr. Smith. Can I get you any more of that Stilton you tried last week?' That is one of our biggest hooks for customers. It feels like family when you come in there."

Customer service at Feast! means just that. They staff the store with friendly people who are food lovers. These are people who want to take care of the customer, give them a basket when their arms get full, and answer questions about herbal-infused vinegars, which may be unfamiliar to some. "One thing that my husband and I feel is very important is not to have a snooty gourmet food store," Kate says. "We look at it like welcoming guests into our home, instead of trying to sell them things. Our goal is not to up-sell. Our goal is to make people feel comfortable so they want to come back regularly."

Feast! has come a long way since its founding in 2002. They expanded the business twice, the first time shortly after they opened with the addition of a gift store. That turned out to be a misstep for them because by adding gifts they shifted their focus away from what made them really special. Ultimately they shrank the gift store back and opened a café instead, which played to their strengths. "That [gifts] was not something that was our specialty, and so it wasn't extremely special. And so we really focused on what was special, which was expanding our meats, expanding our cheese, doing more produce. What really grew the business was adding that plus our café and lunch business."

Instead of offering hard goods, Feast! specializes in food baskets and boxes customizable by the gift giver. And as opposed to offering a pre-selected assortment of items in a gift basket, Feast! gives shoppers their own bag that they can fill up with what they want to put in a basket. "We used to have gift bags that we put together, but customers always wanted to take out a couple of things and add others. But you have to do what the customers want and are asking you for. So now they select their own stuff that we use to make into a basket. This has been a much bigger hit. They feel like they did the shopping, but they didn't have to do everything," Kate says.

They also added Feast! branded items, like their signature pimento cheese, which makes their brand memorable. "For some reason people like to wear the Feast! name on their t-shirt. Customers keep buying our signature shirts and bibs, so we want to carry that as far as we can," Kate adds.

Feast!'s owners Kate and Eric have created a shop that POPs! by delivering an excellent, high-quality product that is special and different from that found in grocery stores, adding the element of customer engagement by encouraging shoppers to taste and try before they buy – "We try to get it into their mouth" – and creating an atmosphere that invites the customers in. "When we designed the store, it was important to us that if we were going to be at this place all the time, we wanted it to feel like a place that we wanted to be. So we wanted to have great music, good lighting, good colors, and a vibrant staff. The staff is really special. They are young food lovers and have lots of creative energy. Fun is one of the things that makes the store have the good energy it has. And when we bake our molasses sugar cookies, the smell makes it comfortable, homey, and tantalizing as well," Kate concludes.

Building Customer Involvement Takes the Right People

Despite all the rhetoric in marketing circles about "belonging" to the brand and "connecting" with the brand, true connection can only occur between and among people. That is why brands that are people brands, brands like Michael Kors, Ralph Lauren, Oprah Winfrey, Martha Stewart, Diane Von Furstenberg, and on and on, are ultimately so much more powerful in the retail marketplace than brands that do not have that personal connection. Those non-personal brands must invest a fortune in advertising and marketing to make a connection, whereas people relate to people, they build community with other people, they get involved with people. It is really hard to feel a personal connection to a thing or a branding concept. People relate to people, they build community with other people, they get involved with people. It is really hard

! People relate to people, they build community with other people, they get involved with people.

to feel a personal connection to a thing or a branding concept.

One of the most powerful elements in a store is the people who wait on you and service you in the store. Clearly, mass merchants with their do-it-yourself shopping philosophy are trying to move away from the up-close and personal touch found in smaller, more personal shopping environments. And this is where specialty independent retailers have an edge.

Shoppers everywhere long for that personal touch and feel nostalgic for the time when the people manning the stores really knew their stuff and could be a resource for the shopper who needs to make sometimes confusing decisions, like "Will my guests prefer this soft goat cheese or the hard cheddar?" How much better life is when someone who really knows cheese – and you completely trust – can authoritatively and confidently recommend, "Let's do this one and that one, and why don't you add the pimento spread for people who might prefer something less stimulating? And can I show you a couple of wines that will pair wonderfully with the cheeses you've selected?" Yes, please! That is the ultimate level of customer involvement in the shopping experience.

How to Create Customer Involvement and Interaction

Shops that POP! create a shopping environment that fully involves the shopper and engages them interactively in the shopping experience. Shoppers don't just browse the aisles and participate as passive observers. Shops that POP! encourage customers to touch, feel, taste, try on, and participate in the store in a more involving way.

Use all five senses.   Stores are well accustomed to using visual merchandising techniques to engage customers, but there are four more senses that can be even more powerful. Let customers hear your signature music while they shop, or choose a fragrance (like freshly baked cookies that they can also taste) that they will associate with you. If you sell food products, be sure that tasting the wares is easy. Place displays where customers can feel the heft of an item and look at all the details. The more senses the customer uses, the more engaged they will be.

Employ your expertise. Don't spread yourself thin by trying to be all things to all people; recognize that customers will come in as much for your expertise as for your product. Suggest a great wine pairing to go with your specialty food items, or help customers create a beautiful wedding bouquet that uses the language of flowers to tell a story. One knowledgeable expert is worth a half-dozen temporary employees who are there for a paycheck and little else.

Let customers wear your brand. Customers love to feel part of a team or a family. If your customers express an interest in shirts, aprons, or baseball caps with your logo, make them available. A satisfied customer wearing your logo is the best advertising you will ever have. And dressing your staff in logo uniforms is also a way to let your customers know who in your shop is there to help.

Chapter 9

Create the Ultimate Customer Experience
Evoke Shopper Curiosity

*"I love it when I catch someone's reaction at my stores,
when they turn a corner and come upon something
unexpected. Maybe it's something they didn't know they
had to have until that moment, or it's the way we've
displayed something that's a little out of the ordinary that
they might be able to use in their decorating."*

—Mary Carol Garrity of Nell Hill's

CURIOSITY may kill the cat, but it brings the shopper to life. Curiosity is what draws shoppers into the store, and pulls them down the aisle and around the corner to find wonderful, exciting, got-to-have things. Owing to our hunter-gatherer roots, people are programmed to notice changes, even subtle shifts, in the environment. Furthermore, because shopping hearkens back to our ancestors' hunting-and-gathering behavior, shops that POP! evoke a powerful curiosity factor that attracts shoppers and keeps them looking – or more correctly, hunting – throughout the store.

Think about the overwhelming curiosity factor that Mary Liz Curtin uses to draw shoppers to Leon & Lulu. The store is housed in a building that from the outside still looks much like its predecessor, the town roller skating rink. And greeters meet the guests on roller skates. Who can pass that up? With extra attention to storefront window displays, Mary Liz tantalizes shoppers to come inside to satisfy their curiosity and see what the excitement is all about.

And once they get inside the real fun starts. As a shopper testifies,

"This is my favorite furniture store in Michigan. You walk in and are overwhelmed by the abundance of furniture of different shapes and sizes. As you wander, you are served drinks and cookies by associates on roller skates (a nod to the building's past life.) The associates are exceedingly helpful and are not on commission." Curiosity is what draws shoppers into the store, and pulls them down the aisle and around the corner to find wonderful, exciting, got-to-have things.

> ! Curiosity is what draws shoppers into the store, and pulls them down the aisle and around the corner to find wonderful, exciting, got-to-have things.

In research with shoppers, we find that merchandise-related features are among the most influential in determining the store where a person wants to shop. Besides things like merchandise quality, wide selection, and unique merchandise and place to shop for many things, shoppers are motivated to find out what is new, different, and interesting. Shoppers respond to stores that change up their merchandise often.

Shoppers are likely to shop more often in stores where merchandise moves in and out quickly. Retailers are rewarded when stock turns frequently because shoppers are powerfully stimulated to buy. Shoppers learn they can't afford to pass something up that they want, because if they wait, it might not be there the next time. As Mary Carol Garrity says of her Nell Hill's shoppers, "People who shop here know that if they see it and they want it, they'd better buy it. It won't be here the next time they come."

However, actual stock movement can be real or virtual, an impression created by simply redoing displays and shifting merchandise around from place to place. Mary Carol calls her displays "my silent salespeople." Included among her staff are dedicated decorators who do nothing but displays all day long, bringing out new stock and moving around existing merchandise. Constantly changing merchandise and displays is one of the prime features that make Nell Hill's POP!

Boxwoods Gardens & Gifts – A Curiously Different Gift Store

From the first moment you see Boxwoods Gardens & Gifts, it evokes curiosity. Located in Buckhead, Georgia, right outside of Atlanta, in a quaint suburban neighborhood, it looks like nothing more than a cottage home, hardly a store. With dense front garden and moss-covered patio, it simply invites you to stroll up the steps, open the front door, and come on inside.

Once you enter, it is more and more curious. In keeping with the cottage feel, the Boxwoods store is broken up into small intimate rooms, each showcasing different assortments of merchandise, like the fashion room and garden room; indeed it has grown to encompass three individual houses. You simply can't stop wandering through, because it is a store made up of nooks and crannies filled to the brim with wonderful stuff.

Dan Belman, co-owner of Boxwoods Gardens & Gifts with his partner Randy Korando, says, "When people walk in, it's either 'welcome to my nightmare,' or 'come on in to the dog-and-pony store.' We started off with just one side of the building, then we added glass conservatories and it grew and grew. My father says 'this is a gruesome business,' meaning we grew some, then we grew some more."

From the beginning Dan and his partner were aiming for a destination shop that was an experience. As a result, the store website, as good as it is, can never convey the nature of the store. "We try to give an image of the shop online, but it's impossible. It's very touchy-feely," Dan says. That "touchy-feely" nature of the store comes from the commitment of its owners and as a result, Boxwoods was named one of the Top 50 Retailers in the U.S. and voted Atlanta's Best Home Accessory, Best Holiday Décor Shop, and Best Garden Gift Shop. With a diversity of offerings, Boxwoods features home accessories, chandeliers and home décor, women's accessories, and live plants. "It's kind of like an old time department store," Belman says.

The store evolved from the partners' landscaping business and today Boxwoods has a booming, if non-traditional, floral business. "We were hoping for a fun and friendly shopping experience that would serve to showcase unusual, one-of-a-kind items and that would also highlight our creative floral abilities."

One of the more curious things about Boxwoods is that they don't sell cut flowers or arranged flower bouquets. They only sell living plants, so all flowers are delivered in pots with their very own greenery. Dan says, "The problem with cut flowers is that they have such a short shelf life. They last a couple of days, if you're lucky a week, then you toss them out. We promote floral compositions, which is basically we take anything from an old sugar bowl, centerpiece, basket, whatever and fill it with plants, both flowering plants and greenery. We have done weddings with live plants that instead of spending $10,000 on flowers that just get thrown out, people wind up with planted compositions that they can take and plant in their yard to create a permanent memory."

With a focus on the unusual and unique, they use antiques and vintage furniture as store fixtures along with antique sconces, chandeliers, and other decorative accents and everything is for sale. "We go to Europe on buying trips three to four times a year," Dan explains about the store's merchandising. "By its very nature, what we bring back is old and antique stuff, so it is one of a kind and unique. And that's what our customers crave. We have what we call the cell phone network. When we get a shipment from Europe in, we don't even have time to get on the phone to call our customers to tell them because one customer will walk in on the morning a container comes in and three hours later we'll have the whole parking lot packed with people, because one girlfriend will call another and another." Now that is powerful word of mouth.

Boxwoods also stocks plenty of new giftware items, taking advantage of their Atlanta location to shop the huge Atlanta wholesale gift show every day it is open from morning till night, over the course of the show's ten-day run. "We go to every showroom we can. We look at everything. We try to find unique stuff and we create our own unique stuff in our plant department," Dan says. Due to the store's heavy sales volume, difficulties in sourcing one-of-a-kind items, and the overall weakness of the dollar in overseas markets, Boxwoods' original plan for an even division among gifts, antiques, and plants has been adjusted toward more emphasis on gifts. "We are big believers in finding product that looks like it should cost twice what it is selling for and that has definitely become part of the culture of our shop," says Dan.

! "We are big believers in finding product that looks like it should cost twice what it is selling for, and that has definitely become part of the culture of our shop."

But no matter what merchandise they are buying for their customers, the guiding principle in Boxwoods' merchandise selection, besides uniqueness, is value. "We're really big on bang for the buck. Both Randy and I by nature are frugal. We live a good lifestyle, but we do it with one eye toward value." Another curious feature that elevates Boxwoods Gardens & Gifts beyond the run-of-the- mill gift shop is a department dedicated to fashion accessories and hand-crafted jewelry. At the suggestion of Chris, one of their longtime employees, they brought in an artist line of garden-themed jewelry. After this first success, they gave over a curio cabinet to Chris to stock up with more jewelry. "From what started in one little case, we've now turned over and devoted a whole room to what we call the girlie-girlie stuff, which is jewelry, handbags, pashminas, cell phone holders. Randy and I don't do any of that buying because we wouldn't know where to begin," Dan says.

Fortunately for them, Chris does, because she has scored a real hit in the fashion accessories department, offering high style and extremely good value. Commenting on the success of fashion sales, Dan says, "We just had somebody come in today and she bought 12 handbags. She found out about them from her friend who told her 'You can't believe the prices on these wonderful handbags.' So she came in and did all of her Christmas shopping for all of her nieces in our handbag department."

It is win-win for Boxwoods Gardens & Gifts, its owners, its employees, and its customers. It starts at the top and works its way throughout the whole atmosphere and culture of the store. "Our best assets are our employees, without question. Through both words and action we try to achieve a friendly and supportive atmosphere with our employees. This feeling that we refer to as being part of the Boxwoods' family is conveyed to our customers, who then feel like friends of the family. Many customers are really our friends. Like at Christmas time when retail is crazy, we have people bring us boxes of cookies or homemade cakes. It is amazing how nice they are that they really feel that we're more than just a store. It is a good feeling for them; it's a good feeling for us. We're a very happy shop."

Evoke Curiosity by Exciting by Changing Things Up

Both Nell Hill's and Boxwoods Gardens & Gifts are in the envious position of moving so much merchandise in and out of the store that getting customers curious about what's in stock is simply a natural outgrowth of that perpetual motion. Speaking of turnover, Dan of Boxwoods says, "We do such a heavy volume for a little shop that things are constantly changing. And it becomes part of a cycle, where things move so quickly, people know that they have to buy it when they see it. And that gives us room to bring in more product. It kind of goes around and comes around."

Other stores have to stimulate that curiosity through other means and that is where imagination and creativity enter the picture, plus hard work. If merchandise is not moving out on its own, by being purchased, retailers should make a regular practice of moving it around themselves. Play with displays; play around with the merchandise. Try out new arrangements. An item that gets lost in one spot could well POP! in another.

How to Evoke Curiosity

Shops that POP! have a curiosity factor. Curiosity is heightened when shoppers are confronted with the unexpected. It's what makes them come in to discover what the excitement is all about. They excite consumer curiosity to explore and experience, from the shop windows and entrance through the different displays. They lure shoppers into the store and then to turn the next corner and walk down the next aisle to find that wonderful treasure just out of sight. They simply have got to go see what is going on inside.

What special invitations to shop does your shop front communicate? Step outside your store and look objectively at what messages your store front says. Does your shop door look like every other one on the block? If so, change it up. Are your windows tired looking, old, in need of a fix? Then update them. Do you have a lot of signs or paperwork cluttering up the door front? Toss them. You only get one chance to make a first impression on customers. Make that first impression POP!

Find something special about your store to shine a spotlight on. Sometimes it is easy to find something special and distinctive about your store, like Leon & Lulu or Boxwoods, but sometimes you have to look harder. Persistence will pay off, if you can find something about your building, your neighborhood, your store selection, your experience, that makes your store a true one-of-a-kind destination. Work hard to make your shop stand out amid your neighbors.

Change the merchandise to change the customers' perceptions and experiences. We have seen how in stores where merchandise moves quickly the rate of turnover is a powerful stimulant to get people to buy. Use that understanding to move things around in your space. Make a regular practice of resetting displays, preferably before the store opens each day, take something and shift it around. Keep things moving to keep sales growing.

Chapter 10

Create the Ultimate Customer Experience

Create a Contagious, Electric Quality in the Store

"We see our customers as invited guests to a party, and we are the hosts. It's our job every day to make every important aspect of the customer experience a little bit better."
— Jeff Bezos, Amazon.com

Nell Hill's has got it. Feast! has got it and Godfrey's has got it in spades. Each store is a shop that POPs! because they built a contagious, electric quality in their stores. The atmosphere is so kinetic it literally draws people into the store to find out what all the excitement is about. And it is contagious because people learn about the store largely through word of mouth, one customer telling another and another about the fun experience of shopping there. True shopping electricity can't be dialed in. Electricity arises organically and spreads throughout to the community to draw people in.

> ! True shopping electricity can't be dialed in. Electricity arises organically and spreads throughout to the community to draw people in.

A lot of retailers try to introduce electricity into the store through music and pulsating rhythms, but that looks a little too desperate. They try with a little paint and polish to rev up the electricity, but that looks contrived.

True shopping electricity, excitement, and contagious quality in a store derive from something far more basic than loud music, blonde wood, stainless steel fixtures, and sans serif fonts. Electricity arises organically and creates a magnetic pull to the shoppers. The electricity we are talking about can't be dialed in; it must arise organically from the store environment itself and spread throughout the community to draw people in.

Clearly creating a shop with high levels of customer involvement and one that evokes shopper curiosity helps build the kinetic quality, but based upon the interviews with shopkeepers, they feel that their shops' electricity originates in the store staff members and then jumps from person to person. People who work in the store are the source of electricity and their energy just radiates outward to spark shoppers and spreads out into the community to make that shop a destination.

When asked what generates the kinetic quality at Boxwoods Gardens & Gifts, Dan Belman says it comes from the salespeople: "Our salespeople are excited about the merchandise we carry and that creates excitement for the customers." Pat McLaughlin of Coventry Corners affirms the need to focus on having the right people staffing the store. "Hiring is key. They are the face of us, so I hire energetic, caring, responsible associates who love being here. From what the staff wears, what we buy, it is all a big package. I hire energetic associates and I empower them." Or at the bakery, restaurant and gift shop devoted to all things "key lime," Kermit's Key West Key Lime Shoppe, where the staff not only sells and serves, but also makes what they sell.

Kermit's Key West Key Lime Shoppe – More than a Tangy Treat, It Delivers a Zestful Shopper Experience

Walk down to the Historic Seaport in Key West, and, among the boat slips and bars, you will find a bright yellow house with green trim. If you are lucky, an effervescent man in a matching chef's uniform – Kermit – will greet you, inviting you into the world of Kermit's Key West Key Lime Shoppe, a shop that sells key lime pies and other key lime items primarily to the tourists who visit the small island of 27,000 residents.

While Kermit's Key Lime Pie is widely regarded as the best there is by Food Network, National Geographic, Paula Deen and others, what makes Kermit's stand out is not its key lime pie, although certainly that is a delicious treat. It's possible to get key lime pie – with or without meringue, with or without whipped cream, on a variety of crusts, or dipped in chocolate – at virtually any eatery in Key West. No, the memorable part of Kermit's is how well the shop reflects the culture of the island in a way that visitors wish to remember.

"Key West is not slick; people come to get away from slick," says Karen Puglisi, sales and marketing director for Kermit's. More than one competitor has failed to understand this basic fact, redressing a store to become sleek, modern – and totally not Key West. In fact, one of Kermit's major competitors rode a willingness to embrace a modern, urban vibe all the way to national media attention, but the result was a store that is cold, sterile, and unwelcoming to the throngs of visitors immersed in the semi-tropical heat, the ambient salsa music, and the mix of architectural styles that characterize Key West. Kermit's, on the other hand, gets the formula right because it is authentic, not contrived.

Tourists come to Key West to experience a culture that they cannot find at home, one that is quirky, individual, and even a bit rebellious. It's no wonder the unofficial motto of the island is, "We're all here because we're not all there." Kermit's fits right in with this attitude of gentle insanity. Kermit himself stands out on the corner, greeting tourists, posing for selfies with children and brides, and pretending to throw key lime pies at the Conch Train tour that runs around the island. "The trolley drivers talk about him," says Puglisi.

Kermit's also understands the appeal of the handcrafted to the Key West market. On an island where businesses think nothing of having their primary branding carried by a sign hand-painted on plywood, competitors miss the mark by having modern, minimalistic signage and marketing collateral. Kermit's, on the other hand, designs and prints all labels in-house (under Puglisi's supervision), featuring a caricature of Kermit himself.

One of the challenges that Kermit's faces is fostering return visits. Many tourists visiting Key West do so as a stop on a Caribbean cruise and may never physically return to the island. Kermit's works with the cruise lines to place advertising in the staterooms, where cruisers constitute a "captive audience," Puglisi says. "We have to get to them before they get to us," she says.

But the ultimate goal is to have these transient visitors maintain a connection to the store. Currently, Kermit's has over 10,000 Facebook fans that enjoy getting regular updates to remind them of their most recent visit to this sub-tropical locale. "Our goal is to have them purchase and then order [again] online," Puglisi says. When customers open that box from Kermit's, they can be sure that they will receive some delicious key lime pie and a taste of the tropics.

Electricity Is the Kinetic Spark that Breeds Success

By harnessing the power of electricity, retailers can see their stores blossom with success, which breeds more success. The fact is, you simply can't make the electricity happen – it must grow organically through a whole combination of factors – and it starts with the people who provide the vital spark. It flows from the top down, from the excitement and enthusiasm of the shop owner to the staff, then ultimately to the shoppers. We've seen that Nell Hill's Mary Carol Garrity never leaves the sale floor. "The energy comes from the love of what you are doing. I think too many people get caught up in the wrong thing. I love being out on the floor. I love working with the customer. I love listening to what they're asking for and what they're saying," Mary Carol says. That kind of enthusiasm simply is contagious.

Pat at Coventry Corners concurs that the passion, enthusiasm and electricity must spring from the top. "Discover your passion, a passion that can meet the needs of people and fill a void. My passion was décor and I love to work with people. I am a teacher with a master's degree in child guidance. I use that training with the 45 people working for us. Frankly, I am a workaholic. I work in the store every day." Pat and her team are the spark electrifying the Coventry Corners experience for the new customer or the customer that is returning time and time again.

Tiger Lily –
A Shop that Blossoms with Beauty and Enthusiasm

While all the retailers interviewed for this book were super-enthused about their business with electricity exuding throughout their interviews, Manny Gonzales from Charleston, South Carolina's Tiger Lily, a flower shop with a difference, stands out in terms of high-voltage electricity. Manny runs Tiger Lily with his wife Clara, who was the flower enthusiast behind the venture. Manny came out of Marriott Hotels as director of catering, so he wasn't weighted down with traditional "florists' think" in running his business. In fact, he claims when he and Clara were operating Tiger Lily in traditional flower-shop mode they were headed for the poorhouse.

"And that's when we said, let's just be Tiger Lily and be the best that we can be and forget all about the rules that we're supposed to follow to be a florist. . . . We decided we were going to be the best place to buy awesome flowers. That's it," says Manny Gonzales. "Originally we didn't know much about the business, but Clara had a flair for it, so we decided we could teach ourselves and scratch out a living. So we followed all the books that told us how to be a florist, and we just weren't that happy. After a couple of years, we had our backs to the wall and almost went out of business. And that's when we said, 'Let's just be Tiger Lily and be the best that we can be.' That's when we got rid of the balloons, the toys, the cards, the plastic buckets, the daisies and the carnations, and somebody taking telephone orders. We decided we were going to be the best place to buy awesome flowers. That's it. So we just brought in the best flowers we could possibly find, got the best designers we could find, and we just try to blow people away every time they walk in the door. We will celebrate our twentieth anniversary next year. We've grown to be the biggest florist in South Carolina, and added a second location in Kiawah Island, South Carolina," Manny says.

> ! [L]et's just be Tiger Lily and be the best that we can be and forget all about the rules that we're supposed to follow to be a florist. . . . Be the best place to buy awesome flowers.

For many florists the wire services are their lifeline and source of new business. But for Manny it was the kiss of death. "The best payoff we got was withdrawing from the wire services where you pick a picture out of the book. To me it was our major source of mediocrity, and mediocrity is a four-letter word around here. We try to be different. We try to be awesome. How can you do that when you're following a book? How can you be special and different if you're doing what everybody else is doing?" Manny explains.

In cutting the umbilical cord to the florists' business that the wire services represent, they were left to stand on their own, create their own unique vision in order to grow their business. It was a brave and bold move, but one that has paid off many times over for Tiger Lily as they morphed from being an ordinary run-of-the-mill florist, to being flower superstars.

"The quality of what we were doing just took off because when you sent an arrangement out that had Tiger Lily on it; it wasn't a picture from a book. It was the vision of a designer. And the customer says, 'That's cool, that's different.' It immediately separated Tiger Lily from what everybody else was doing. And it really gave us the freedom to do whatever we believed in, and that's our vision, which is 'killer flowers' and 'killer service' that goes above and beyond, exceeding your expectations every time," Manny continues.

These are quite ambitious goals but their track record attests to the fact that Tiger Lily is doing it. They have been voted Best Florist in Charleston every year since 2000. The Charleston Metro Chamber of Commerce recognized Tiger Lily as one of the "2004 Emerging 10 Companies" and followed up with the "2004 Small Business of the Year" Award. In 2005, Manny and Clara Gonzales were selected as Runner-Up for the South Carolina "2005 Small Business Person of the Year Award" presented by the SC Small Business Administration. *Florist Review Magazine* recognized Tiger Lily as "2006 Runner Up Retail Florist of the Year" and The Knot brides have picked Tiger as Best of Weddings since 2007. In 2009 Clara Gonzales was a finalist in the CEO Category for the Influential Women in Business presented by the Charleston Regional Business Journal. *Elegant Bride* magazine said Tiger Lily is "one of America's Best Wedding Flower Designers," and they were featured in *Southern Living* magazine in December 2005 in South Carolina People and Places.

With those accolades confirming their strategy, they decided to use their rewards as the key message to build the brand identity for Tiger Lily. Manny says, "That gave us the confidence to say, 'I'm not going to say we're the best because we try to be as good as we can be every day.' But if you [the customers] are saying we are the best, then I'm going to let that be known. So we put that on our vans, in our sale collateral, on our labels. And people started calling us because they wanted the best in town. There was a real need for special attention, special flowers, and special focus on what people say is important. Our sales have just gone through the roof every year since."

The electricity at Tiger Lily comes partly from this iron-willed commitment to being the best of the best, but it also comes from the electricity of being surrounded by flowers upon entering the store. "When people come in our front door, they basically run into 2,000 flowers. You smell them. You can touch them. You can pick them up. There is a whole floral kaleidoscope around you," Manny says.

He goes on to describe the energy in Tiger Lily's flower studio like that found in a gourmet restaurant. "If you were to stop and think about a florist, you'd probably think of a quiet, peaceful place. But around here is it like walking into a kitchen of a five-star restaurant and all the energy. That's why people buy flowers. They're not buying flowers so much for the colors. They're buying the energy. And we want them to get a taste of that energy when they come in."

As an encouragement for shoppers to come into the store and partake of that floral-energy boost, Tiger Lily offers a half-price discount on all flowers shoppers pick out and buy for themselves.

Perhaps one of the most challenging aspects of Tiger Lily's business, yet what makes them draw deep within their own creative reserves, is the customized nature of their business. Each design is unique, depending upon the needs of the customer, what flowers are available that day, how much they want to spend, and the creativity of the designer. "Value is a real buzz word for us. We're not the cheapest, but we want to be the best and offer the best value. Because I come from a food and beverage background, I see lots of parallels between the two businesses. Most florists out there are offering cheap fast food, but people want gourmet dining. We want to be the gourmet florist. The value's there because we aren't making floral arrangements, we are fulfilling your floral fantasies. People will spend $250 on an arrangement and call us the next day to say how unbelievable it was."

So Tiger Lily delivers great product and great customer experiences, but behind it all is the dedication, creativity and passion of the Tiger Lily staff. Manny and Clara feel their amazing staff is the reason for their success. "We feel truly blessed to have such a wonderful team, to work with incredible flowers, in this spectacular town."

Electricity Starts with the People Then Spreads from There

Electricity gives a store its soul, and electricity only comes from the people. With all the energy emitting from Tiger Lily, Manny credits his people as the ultimate source of his shop's electricity. "I think the number one thing that I do is I hire people who are truly engaged in what they do—people who can work with flowers for eight hours, and then have a box of flowers come in and still say, 'wow, that's beautiful.' Even after a full day, they still have that passion. And that energy really sets a standard for the other designers in the shop, and they feed off of it. So there's a lot of energy back there [in the design room]. And then again I like to have folks come in the back room and get a wisp of that energy."

Ultimately it's the people that make a shop that POPs! – hire the wrong people, or even choose the wrong retail focus for yourself as an owner, and you will cut the necessary electricity off at the source. Choose the right people and your passion for your business, however, and you will generate the power you need to stay in shoppers' minds long after they walk out your door.

How to Generate Electricity

Building a feeling of excitement and electricity is critical to the success of your store, drawing customers in time and again. Do your shoppers feel that immediate burst of electricity the moment they set foot on your store property? Here are some tips for creating a spark:

Surround yourself with people who are as passionate about your store as you are. Your store employees are the "power lines" that will carry the electricity to your customers. Be extra-selective when you choose an employee for your store; it's far better to wait for a person who projects excitement and enthusiasm, than to simply hire to fill an open shift. Train your staff so they are comfortable and confident presenting your product line. Make working as much fun as possible, both for yourself and your staff, to keep the electricity flowing. How can you energize and electrify your staff each and every day so that they energize and electrify the customers as well?

Sell only the items you are most passionate about. Just as the owners of Tiger Lily found out, it is far more important to sell a smaller array of "gourmet" items than to "stick to the book" and sell what people expect you to sell. Leave those every day, boring, expected items for other retailers, while you concentrate on only those items that make you and your staff excited to share with shoppers. No doubt, there are products, product lines, even whole sections of your store that are not paying their freight. Make those disappear and try something new and different. What products are holding you back, not making your store sparkle?

Draw on the electricity of your environment. Kermit's Key West Key Lime Shoppe has mastered the art of channeling the electric environment of their area while still standing out among other retailers. Take a cue from Kermit's and learn why potential customers visit your area, then be sure to channel that specific "flavor" of electricity to those who come to your store. For Kermit's, it is bright tropical colors, a casual environment, and a certain spontaneity. What makes your area unique?

Chapter 11

Create the Ultimate Customer Experience

Converge Atmosphere, Store Design and Merchandise

"The car, the furniture, the wife, the children – everything has to be disposable. Because you see the main thing today is shopping."

—Arthur Miller

Shops that POP! have a multi-dimensional quality. Everything about the store – its atmosphere, its design, its merchandise offerings, its staff – converge to tell a unique story for the customer. That special story is its soul, the store's DNA, and it is reflected through every touchpoint in the store. The store environment is unified by the design, layout, architectural elements, space, and paths through the store, and the atmosphere of the store, including lighting, music, and scent. These factors connect naturally with the merchandise offered, including how it is displayed, presented, organized, and offered for sale.

Through an emphasis on these more or less objective physical elements that characterize a store, shop owners can exert a powerful influence on shoppers in order to touch them emotionally and influence them to buy. However, there is an elusive, transcendent quality to this connection between the physical and emotional, which is where the magic happens.

! An elusive, transcendent quality to the connection between the physical and emotional is where the magic happens.

Whenever a question comes up related to the physical design of a store environment the go-to guy Unity Marketing turns to is architect Ken Nisch, chairman of JGA, a Southfield, Michigan–based group that has become one of the nation's leading retail design, brand strategy, and architectural firms. With a client list a mile long, including such retailers as Hot Topic, Diesel, Godiva Chocolatier, J.Jill, Levenger, Brookstone, Mikasa, Saks Department Store Group, Rainforest Café, Coca-Cola, The North Face, Hershey's, and Tommy Hilfiger to name a few, Ken describes his firm as "a retail branding and environmental design company that focuses on transactional companies, such as retail stores, restaurants, theme parks, airline terminals, banks, and hospitals – anyplace where money and experience or products changes hands." That means he is concerned with far more than buildings or the bricks and mortar traditionally associated with architecture, but with all retailing touchpoints and experiences.

Ken explains what makes this convergence factor between the atmosphere, the design, and the merchandise work in the retail environment is when the store is "full of places that unexpectedly meet your expectations, versus an environment like Gap which is full of expected places that meet your expectations. The key is to create environments filled with places of unexpected difference just to keep the customer engaged." This paradoxical idea of meeting shoppers' expectations by creating the unexpected is what extraordinary stores like Boxwoods Gardens & Gifts, Tiger Lily, Nell Hill's, and STORY have done.

Ken describes this as paradox environments, as opposed to parallel environments, where the shopper has come to expect the expected and as a result is overcome with boredom. "Customers are increasingly fatigued with parallel environments. I think of Ralph Lauren or Talbots as being parallel – the store, the merchandise, the marketing, the branding are all absolutely consistent. Versus a store like Anthropologie, which is an example of the paradoxical in retail – relatively expensive merchandise in a flea market environment so you can create a mix-and-match look. You never see a table in the middle with one sweater in four different colors with pants to match, such as at Talbots. In Anthropologie you see fashion and home together with things mix and match, all different sizes, and accessories hanging around. It makes you feel like you discovered the environment. Shoppers who openly seek self-expression through shopping feel that they created the outfit, rather than it was created

! Retailers need to offer
• the unexpected in
interesting, stimulating,
and exciting ways.

for them. This explains why retailers like The Gap are having such a tough time – they don't offer their shoppers creativity or self-expression." The future success of retailers will be found when they offer the unexpected in interesting, stimulating, and exciting ways.

It takes a certain kind of shopper to thrive in these paradoxical environments. They must have confidence and sophistication in order to put the look together and create their own self expression, as opposed to shopping in a parallel environment where it is all put together for you. Therefore, the Doyle & Doyle or Nell Hill's or STORY experience isn't for everyone, but just right for that special customer. Increasingly in today's consumer-empowered marketplace, shoppers are rising to the challenge that a paradox environment presents. They are more knowledgeable, more experienced, more sophisticated.

Yesterday's shoppers might have wanted the comfort and confidence that parallel environments, like Talbots or Gap, offered, but today they want something more. The future success of retailers will be found when they offer the unexpected in interesting, stimulating, and exciting ways.

Shoppers Hate Clutter, but They Love Discovering Treasures among the Trash

Paradox is the meaning behind the words when you talk to shoppers about what they like and dislike in a shopping environment. While they overwhelmingly hate clutter in a store, they want to shop in an environment that offers them lots to see, lots to explore, lots of stuff; in other words, they want lots of good clutter, instead of bad clutter. Department stores in general, and Macy's in particular, are among the leading culprits in filling up their stores with bad clutter.

Talking about her experience shopping in Macy's, Sharon, a 40-something affluent shopper, says:

"One problem I have [when shopping at Macy's], is how many items of clothing can they shove on a floor rack? You go into Nordstrom, and there's six shirts hanging on a rack, but you go into Macy's and on the same rack you find 75. This is just organized chaos.... They could be the same exact pieces of clothing, but if they are all shoved in there, the clothes are all over and look messy.... It's a turnoff. It almost feels like a fire sale."

In Macy's with their overcrowded racks, she can't discern what the store really is all about. "I like to go into a department store and go to the section I am interested in and browse it without having to fight to make room. I like to know that if I walk in, I can see what they have and then decide whether to stay or not."

No wonder, then, that malls and shopping centers filled with parallel shopping environments are losing shoppers while main streets and independents that offer another, paradox shopping experience are thriving.

The Store Is about Creating Points of Customer Interaction

Designing a store is ultimately about creating points of customer interaction with the products for sale. Ken distinguishes between passive interaction and a more active, involving interaction that ultimately leads the customer toward self-expression and creativity. "Some categories have what I call passive interaction, so for example if I am buying a flat screen television there is a more passive interaction than if I am buying a fragrance that I touch, and feel, put on, and smell. It's the difference between a more personal purchase and one that is about self-expression, as opposed to a television, which is mostly about receiving output." He points to the new way cosmetics are sold – at the end of the counter, rather than across the counter – as one of the more important trends in customer involvement.

Ken continues, "The simple things are going to be more important in the future, like how to get somebody to pick it up, try it on, and react to trying it on. In recent work we did in the cosmetics area we found that the best way to shape and organize the transaction isn't over the counter, but it is best done off the corners of the counter, where the sales person stands next to or beside the customer. [*Note:* "Over the counter" in this case refers to the traditional means of selling to customers across a display counter with the salesperson behind and the customer in front.] This increases the potential of somebody interacting with you. It's going to radically change businesses that have been traditionally done over the counter, including jewelry or cosmetics. We even see it in restaurants where they put the kitchen out front versus hidden in the back. People don't want the beginning and the end. They want to see the middle," Ken says.

"If the sale involves self-expression or creativity, you want to design lots of interactivity. If it doesn't involve self-expression, you may not find interactivity as highly effective in increasing customer interest," Ken suggests. But even in more passive interaction stores, where touching, feeling, experiencing the products is not predominant, art galleries for example, retailers still need to design the environment to increase customer involvement.

People Add the Life into Retail

While Ken's firm designs shopping spaces that create an atmosphere that builds interactivity with the product, the success of bringing these elements together, to make a truly distinctive shopping environment, is ultimately all about the people who fill the space. Commenting on the vital force that people play in the shopping environment, Ken says, "Think of the Apple Store. The environment in itself isn't very interesting if you went into the store before it opens. But what is interesting is what happens when the store opens. It brings people together. They are full of people who want to get their Apple fix and they want to be around other people who are getting their Apple fix, too. So they have become a kind of cultural magnet. It's become something like a club and that is a new category in retail. It used to be that lifestyle retail was considered the ultimate. But now it is concept retail, shops like American Girl Place or Apple or Selfridges. These are stores that are on top of the retail pyramid that have built a community. You become part of the community." "As we need less or want less, stores that figure out how to make you go there – where buying becomes secondary to the experience but not the focus of the experience – are going to be important places," says Ken Nisch, JGA.

The ultimate trick for retail shopkeepers, designers, and planners according to Ken is to draw people to the store for the experience, rather than just to shop. Shopping becomes part of or in addition to the experience. He says, "The argument becomes 'I go, therefore I buy,' rather than 'I buy, therefore I go.' As we need less or want less, stores that figure out how to make you go there – where buying becomes secondary to the experience but not the focus of the experience – are going to be important places. It's what Starbucks has figured out. Buying a cup of coffee is just the price of admission to the experience which is the community. And it is what Apple has. Apple Stores really don't have that much to buy, but they are packing the aisles so full of people you can't even walk through. And the end results is the Apple Stores are doing huge amounts of business on top of it all."

❗Stores where buying becomes secondary to the experience, but not the focus of the experience, are going to be important places.

In much the same way, Dirt Road Divas draws people to the store for the experience, with the purchase of its fashion offerings following, according to owner Jodie Robinson.

Dirt Road Divas –
Where Girls with a Country Heart Find Fashion with City Flair

Jodie Robinson may seem like an unlikely business owner when one hears the story of how she came to Dirt Road Divas, a quirky little clothing boutique near Houston, Texas, that focuses on regional favorites with a Texas twang.

"My husband just bought it!" she laughs. At the time, Robinson was employed as a social worker and was traveling every week. One week she came home to find that her husband had purchased the shop from the original owners, who had apparently found that retail was not the relaxing pastime they had hoped for.

The original years were a challenge. Robinson and her husband had to learn the business from the ground up, and along the way, they have evolved some innovative ways of creating a store environment using the principles of convergence to create a shopping environment combining store design and atmosphere, unique merchandise, storytelling displays and highly trained and customer-focused staff to make Dirt Road Divas memorable for the customers and that draws them back for more.

It all starts with the store name. "Mix in a bit of country, a little Texas twang, some Southern Charm, pour in some glitz and glimmer and there you have it: A Dirt Road Diva!" the website declares.

"The concept of Dirt Road Divas is that even if you grew up or still live on a dirt road . . . you can love the lat-est styles and wear adorable clothes," Jodie explains. "You can drive your Chevy all day and hop into a limo for a night out on the town," which is exactly what Jodie offered when the store first opened.

One of their original events was the limousine party, in which a women's group might work with the store to allow a group to be picked up in a limo, served wine and hors d'oeuvres at arrival, and treated to an evening of shopping. This was a particularly good approach when DRD was in its original location, which could not be seen from the road. Although they have discontinued these parties in their new, smaller-but-better-located site, they are considering reinstituting a new form of after-hours party that will accomplish a similar goal.

But you don't have to arrive by limo to appreciate the uniqueness of DRD. "We're in a location with two other boutiques; we have to stand out to get customers into the shop," Robinson says. She does this with charming displays that allow customers to feel like they are discovering something new every time they walk in.

! We're in a location with two other boutiques; we have to stand out to get customers into the shop. They need to feel like they are discovering something new every time they walk in.

"We try to make the store different from anything you've ever seen," she says. That includes using a lot of vintage pieces in lieu of display racks. At DRD, an antique cigarette machine is used to hang jewelry from, inviting customers to come and touch and remember. Robinson also spent countless hours stoning an old saddle with rhinestones, and now customers come just to take pictures of their children on this sparkly seat.

The product selection is also unique to DRD. Robinson works with local small wholesalers to provide items that would be hard to find outside the Houston area. A local candle manufacturer developed a custom scent called "Dirt Road Divas" that is available only in the store.

Additionally, Robinson is not shy about involving her customers in product selection. She regularly displays samples on her Facebook page and asks her customers which they would order if they had the call. Such posts attract lots of comment from customers who are clearly her regulars, who also post that they are coming right in to the store to purchase once Robinson says the item has arrived.

Robinson is not above taking advice from the experts. Her store was featured on MSNBC's "Your Business," and in her episode business guru Paco Underhill made suggestions about how to better entice customers to purchase, such as putting an entire look on a mannequin or making sure one pair of jeans faces out on a wall full of jeans, much as one faces a book on a shelf so customers can see the cover amidst a sea of spines.

She also keeps her staff involved in this continual merchandising challenge, encouraging them to change the displays regularly so frequent visitors will feel they are encountering something new in the store when they visit. Holidays and special events are great times for this to happen, which, for DRD, includes Christmas, Fourth of July, and rodeo season!

Robinson encourages other small store owners to find their own path to retail success. "Don't try to compare yourself to other boutiques; it's OK to check out what they have, but try to be different," she says. She also encourages store owners to "think of things you would like as a customer."

Above all, it is the experience that brings people to DRD and to other small stores, Robinson says. "You cannot compete with Amazon," she says, echoing other small store owners who have learned how easy it is for customers to fall back on the ease of online retail. But, Robinson has found that bringing all the diverse pieces together to create a unique shopping experience – like a special scent in the store, a cute shopping bag stuffed with tissue paper for purchases, and even a photo on a rhinestone-accented saddle – will often bring customers back.

How to Create Convergence

Shops that POP! present a comprehensive vision that captures all the tangible and intangible elements of the store into a unified whole. This quality of convergence extends far beyond a cookie-cutter, homogenized, neutralized shopping environment. These shops present a distinctive point of view that tie together all the disparate elements of the store into one experience and make it a truly special place to shop.

Does your store and all its many customer touchpoints reflect the holistic DNA that makes your store special, different and unique? Here are some tips for presenting convergence.

Tell a story in every display and in your windows that reflects your vision. Take a walk outside, refresh your eye and then turn back to look at your windows and your displays from the customers' point of view. Do they tell a story that excites the eye, makes them curious, encourages them to want to know more? Are there interesting and different elements that at first might not go together, but yet work well together? What disparate things can you put together to tell a new story? Challenge yourself to bring a new point of view to what your customers see and encounter upon their first step inside the door.

Make the most of the unexpected surprise. Delight your customers with an unexpected surprise, a product line that may be an "outlier" or that doesn't seem to fit, but paradoxically does, like Dirt Road Divas' signature-scented candles in a fashion boutique. Create such unexpected surprises by finding product lines to mix and match in unexpected ways. What surprise can you find for your customers that will reinforce the story you tell your customers, but in a new and different way?

Change it up, move it around, try something different. Let's face it, rearranging a store and all its merchandise is big work, but it can pay off big time by presenting a new, unexpected and different story to your customers. Move things out of the back and put them front row and center to see if changing their location can change sales results. While putting the most purchased items in the back of the store might work in grocery stores, forcing shoppers to navigate the aisles to get to the milk, it doesn't work in specialty stores. Don't force your shoppers to go to the back for the best-selling lines, but also don't pile them all up front so as to negate the fun of exploring. Sprinkle the goodies around, and make sure to provide cues and clues throughout the store to encourage customers to explore. Which lines can you move to the front to give new visibility? Which items in the front can be shifted back to entice shoppers to dig deeper next time they stop in?

Use light, sound, scent, color to tell your story and keep it fresh. Sometimes "shabby" can be chic, but sometimes it is just plain shabby. Don't let this happen in your store. If there are holes in the walls left from old displays, dingy walls in need of a fresh coat of paint, a musty or stale smell, elevator muzak in the background, light bulbs out, dust on the shelves or dirt on the floors or other easily overlooked but essential housecleaning tasks, address them now. Because you are in the store every day, you might miss these signs of inattention, but your customers won't. Same goes for your staff members, if they are unkempt or fashion-challenged, help them step it up for the sake of your profits.

Chapter 12

Create the Ultimate Customer Experience
Create an Authentic Concept

"Capital isn't that important in business. Experience isn't that important. You can get both of these things. What is important is ideas."

—Harvey S. Firestone

Among those qualities that characterize a shop that POPs! – one that makes a true emotional connection with the shopper – is the realization of an authentic vision for the store that works for today and can carry the store into the future. It requires an adherence and strict dedication to the original concept, but it must also allow for growth, change, modification, and adjustment as needed. It's how Manny Gonzales of Charleston, South Carolina's Tiger Lily can throw out the rulebook on how to operate a florist shop in order to be "the best place to buy awesome flowers." It's why Kate Collier's Feast! in Charlottesville, Virginia, can abandon its expansion into a traditional gift business to remain grounded in what they do best: artisanal cheese and meats that also make great gifts.

Prairie Edge –
Where the Shopper Experiences a Vanishing Culture

Located in Rapid City, South Dakota, just a hop, skip, and a jump away from Mount Rushmore and its flag-waving red, white, and blue vision of American history, is Prairie Edge Trading Company & Galleries which honors an entirely different tradition, that of

Native Americans. Prairie Edge invites you to touch, feel, explore, and discover the native culture that was almost lost to us and that even today clings close to the edge of survival.

Prairie Edge has a vital role to play in supporting and building that native culture by offering Native American reproductions, crafts, and craft supplies, Native American-themed books and authentic tribal music, and original art for sale. Prairie Edge, in turn, pays a fair market price to the native craftsmen and women who supply the store with these unique, often rare, and precious items. Prairie Edge was founded in the early 1980s by Ray Hillenbrand and his wife Rita, who turned to raising buffalo on their cattle ranch because the native animals were better suited to the harsh South Dakota environment. This sparked Ray's interest in the traditions and culture of the Northern Plains Indians, which ultimately became Prairie Edge. Today it's a member of the Indian Arts and Crafts Association whose stated mission is "to promote, preserve and protect authentic American Indian arts and crafts."

Describing how that mission is transformed into the retail environment, Prairie Edge's general manager Dan Tribby says, "We are a retail store, so we need to pay our bills, but half of our mission is the ability to educate the visiting public. We're a museum where you get to touch. We're certainly a retail outlet, but it is more than that . . . we're a spiritual store with a museum feeling to it."

> ❗ "We're a museum where you get to touch. We're a retail outlet, but it is more than that . . . we're a spiritual store with a museum feeling to it."

But the educational experiences don't take place just from viewing the artifacts. The Prairie Edge staff members are also entrusted with that role. "We are constantly educating ourselves because not only do we have customers who come in who need to learn, but we do tour groups for bus companies and we do a tremendous number of school tours that come through. There are so many old ideas about Native American culture that are false, that we feel it's our responsibility to give people an idea of what Native American culture really is, both as far as traditional native culture and modern Native American culture as well. Our employees are the driving force in the company, both the staff people and the artists we employee, who have a tremendous amount of freedom to express their vision."

Along with Prairie Edge's dedication to promoting and preserving the native culture is an unwavering respect for the artifacts and items they sell. Prairie Edge isn't just selling objects; they are selling pieces of history and art. "In all the years I have worked here, we've had things come in to make available to the public that you swear are the best of the best. It's just something so above and beyond that you feel bad even putting a price tag on it. And while our job is to sell those best of the best things, you almost don't want them to be sold because you want everyone who comes in to have the opportunity to see something that fantastic. It goes beyond a business-customer relationship. This is all about family and all about friends. Our customers appreciate when we let them know that this is something worth viewing, even if they have no interest in buying it. There's zero pressure to sell it to any individual," Dan explains.

The store's atmosphere and design furthers the shoppers' personal experience with Native American culture. They play native music in the background and throughout the day some of the staff members burn sage in a small ceremony to take out negative energy. The result is that shoppers have a multi-sensory experience of the sights, sounds, and smells that typify the native experience.

Dan says, "When you walk in the door, the visual presentation is absolutely overwhelming. But as a person continues to go through the building, and we have three floors in a National Historic Register building dating from 1886, every one of your senses is tapped. So you might come to an area with a strong smell of smoke from the leather artifacts. And the candle room is filled with the tannic smell of medicinal plants. It is a whole assault on your senses. And it makes people want to learn more because when the customer asks the questions, they have a real interest so there is an opportunity to expand their knowledge. With so much to see and experience in the store, we will have people who spend three or four hours here and they say as they are leaving, 'We'll be back tomorrow because we didn't see it all.'"

> **!** Every one of your senses is tapped. It is a whole assault on your senses. And it makes people want to learn more.

However, Prairie Edge's mission doesn't stop at its front door, but extends out into the community of Rapid City, as well. The company has been instrumental in bringing about a revitalization of downtown Rapid City through the creation of a Main Street Square, a public space that features community events, arts-and-crafts, live concerts, even a skating rink in season. The Main Street Square is surrounded by independently-owned galleries and boutiques in historic buildings, many of which were acquired and restored by the Hillenbrands, the Prairie Edge owners.

To their four neighboring buildings, they set out to install 18 different shops. Ray Hillenbrand explains their goal to fill those vacant slots with local shopkeepers, not national chains, with the same vision for Rapid City as they had. "We found that they were wonderful people with good ideas, and we wanted them to be a team. We told each of them that the idea wasn't for us to make money but for them to add something to the community."

For the future, Prairie Edge is committed to not just looking back at the historical native culture, but to helping propel native artists and craftspeople into the future with a viable outlet for their artwork. "We are blessed to have artists who are so historically correct in what they do, but we also have some fairly young artists too. This new group of native artists is offering less traditional and more contemporary pieces, which are very exciting. It is important for the next generation to step in and get involved with the arts too. So we are always looking, including the employees, for new artists with enough differences in their styles to just keep it shaken up and fascinating for our customers."

The Vision Gives Soul to the Store and Makes It Important to the Customers

All the shopkeepers interviewed for this book express big visions, yet they execute those big visions in very small incremental steps, day in and day out, giving those visions life, body, and soul. For Manny and Clara Gonzales in Charleston, South Carolina, it means the difference between being a florist – a worthy cause and perfectly acceptable vision for a retail shop, but not a concept that POPs! – versus the kind of retail vision that they have created, which is to help customers celebrate important milestones and events in their lives with flowers.

For Barb Emmett and Godfrey's–Welcome to Dogdom it means

to enhance people's relationships with their pets by educating and sharing "the best of the best" for their dogs, not just being a store that sells dog food and accessories. Barb describes the big vision as, "It's not about what is on the shelves, but it is about romancing what's on the shelves. Ultimately it's my passion. I've got to tell people this. I've got to share it with people."

These are the kinds of big visions that lead to longevity and true success. As Ken Nisch of design firm JGA stressed in Chapter 11, "You've got to build a reason for people to be there, and then they will shop. But shopping CAN'T be the reason to be there." The vision or the concept becomes the reason to be there and it's got to have authenticity and value far beyond simply selling stuff.

! "You've got to build a reason for people to be there, and then they will shop. But shopping CAN'T be the reason to be there."

At its heart, a shop has to do something truly important and meaningful for the shopper.

How to Create Authenticity

Striving for more authenticity, pushing the envelope, and expanding the boundaries from a store that sells stuff into something much more meaningful is one of the secrets of transforming a plain vanilla store into one that POPs! It is in recognizing that nobody needs any of the stuff you are selling anyway that the shop owner finds the freedom to explore the boundaries of what a store can aspire to be. It's not about selling clothes, but helping the customer achieve a personal style. It's not selling a flower arrangement, but the very ultimate in floral expression. It's not selling Indian knickknacks, but presenting the unique story of the native peoples through art and artifacts.

That is the kind of vision that inspires the shopkeepers who create shops that make a true, lasting, and deeply meaningful connection with the shoppers. It's the vision that gives people a reason to come to the store and experience the store, so that they can, as a by-product of being there, also shop and do their part in perpetuating the vision for the next generation of shoppers.

Define a mission beyond selling stuff. If you haven't already written a mission statement, do so now; and if you have, study it once again to make sure it expresses an idea beyond selling things.

Your shop must provide something meaningful and important to your customers and your community.

Put your mission front and center in every customer touchpoint. You must live and breathe your mission in everything you do and say to your customers and your staff. Make sure the mission statement is clearly expressed on your store's "About Us" website page. Evaluate all the products you carry, all the signs in your store, and all the displays in your window based upon that mission. Make it your mission to communicate your store's mission every day, in every way.

Focus the mission on your ultimate experience. And while the mission must reflect your values and your ideals, make sure the mission is not all about you. Translate it into what your mission means to your customers. Put it in terms of what experiences your store ultimately delivers to your customers – in other words, what you do for them, not what you sell to them.

Chapter 13

Create the Ultimate Customer Experience

Set Your Price/Value Model
to Favor the Shopper

"People don't necessarily want to spend less – they want to pay less."

—Ken Nisch, JGA

Figuring out an effective price/value model in a retail business can be a formidable stumbling block. It is not easy to price merchandise low enough to make shoppers take notice, yet high enough so the shopkeeper can pay the rent, buy more merchandise, cover payroll and employee benefits, pay the taxes, and then take home a little something extra for themselves – also known as profit.

It is no wonder that finding the right price/value model is difficult, because shoppers are so profoundly confused and confusing. On the one hand, everybody hears about the boom in the luxury market and how retailers offering up goods at the very top of the pricing pyramid are making money hand over fist. However, Unity Marketing has studied the luxury market in depth since 2002 and our research does not support such a view. Luxury retailing is just as difficult and challenging as any other kind of specialty retailing, no matter what the popular media report.

At the other end of the spectrum, specialty retailers feel the pinch from the discount and "big box" retailers, everyone from Walmart, Kmart, Target, and the rest, to the dollar stores, outlet centers, and all the other retailers that ostensibly offer up more for less. The fact is mass marketers through their constant use of discounts and sales to stimulate shoppers have trained customers to wait for sales and look for bargains.

However, for all those retailers who feel that the only way to compete is to sell on the cheap, we say nonsense! You simply aren't working hard enough to give shoppers other reasons to visit your store and buy your stuff. Discount prices have become the one-size-fits-all retailing strategy that has spread throughout the retail landscape. It is dumbed-down retailing. Sure, if you make it cheap enough, somebody likely will buy it, but that isn't good business. Few retailers can match the deep discounts available to mass merchants who can buy in bulk, ship stock out of a central warehouse, and benefit from the volume. The majority of retailers are stuck trying to eke out a living in a world gone mad for the cheap.

Give Shoppers Other Reasons to Shop beyond Cheap: Give them More Value

Here's a suggestion: give shoppers more reasons to shop rather than the promise of cheap. That other reason should be added value. Delivering more value for the money they spend is what works for the ideal customers for your specialty store. You want to attract more affluent customers who have discretion to spend if the value is there, not the discount-oriented or lower-income customers who need to shop discount because their limited budgets necessitate cutting every corner. For higher-income shoppers on which independent specialty retailers depend, retailers need to think of the price/value relationship as a simple three-to-two ratio. That is, give your customers three times more value over the ordinary, everyday brand they can find at discount, but only charge them two times the everyday, discount price. It's a pricing strategy that is simple and easy, and it works. Ultimately shoppers want to spend less, but get more.

And your customers aren't fools. They know what things are worth, especially the affluent who take shopping and spending seriously. What they really want is what looks like a $100 item, actually priced at $75. Sure, some people will only buy that thing if it is marked down a couple of times over, but many more will recognize that if the price is too cheap, then it might not be worth paying for at any price. People know that there is a price for value and shopkeepers need to turn their focus to delivering more value, not necessarily offering up the cheapest price.

When it comes to developing a pricing strategy for a retail store today, it isn't about the money but the meaning and the meaning is delivered through the value of the product. We need to keep the customer's view of the price in mind. If someone wants something badly enough, he or she will pay for it. The key is to make them want it badly enough. Making sure the products you offer are really worth the price is critical, but so is making sure the customer understands the true value that the product price represents.

As *Mad Men*'s Don Draper said, "If you don't like what is being said, then change the conversation," and when it comes to the asking price for your goods, change the conversation to value. A specialty retailer who knows how to hold that value conversation is Ivan Barnett, who with his wife Allison, operates the Patina Gallery in Santa Fe, New Mexico.

Patina Gallery – Romancing the Client

Located since 1999 in a town famous as a destination for working artists and the collectors that covet their work, Patina Gallery has established a reputation for excellence and service in Santa Fe's museum district, filled with many other art galleries. Ivan has lived through the ups and downs of a changing economy, as well as the ups and downs of what's hot and what's not in art gallery circles. But he maintains a long-term vision that has served him well. Indeed the gallery was so named with an appreciation for the historical and cultural context in which it operates, as he explains, "We have a formula that we feel describes the quality we seek in the works that we exhibit, 'Patina = Beauty over Time.' This might apply to Santa Fe as much as to the works we select and love."

Distinctive among Santa Fe's gallery offerings, Patina specializes in large scale mixed-media objects of clay, wood, sculpture and fiber, which combine perfectly with smaller-scaled studio jewelry. As working artists as well as gallery owners, this allows Ivan and Allison to use their gallery space as a "canvas" on which to create a unique artistic vision crafted from the variety of art pieces on display to engage the customer with different textures, scales, colors and surfaces.

Ivan says, "We think that being artists ourselves is important to the Patina style. The gallery's atmosphere is as important to us as the art we exhibit. Our mission is to transport the visitor into our personal world of taste and style. Our canvas is the space itself, and the objects and jewelry are our palette."

Barnett attributes Patina's success to several factors. First is location. While the store has a website, it is the physical location in the museum district that draws in the desired target market. With tourism such a big draw for Santa Fe, managing the seasonality of the ebb and flow of customers can be a challenge. "Black Friday for us is July 1. Then we have an amazing intensity of business. After that, it gets really tricky," Ivan explains. Patina's "Black Friday" comes right before the big tourist season for Santa Fe starts, with the Santa Fe Opera season, the Santa Fe International Folk Art Market and the ART Santa Fe fair.

To bolster business during the off seasons, Patina Gallery connects with groups and organizations traveling to the southwest and organizes private gallery functions for them. He explained that for one such doctors' association group, they closed the store to the public for two hours and brought in a caterer. "These kind of specialized events help offset the decline in the normal brick and mortar high season walk-in. It's taken a lot of years to develop the vocabulary and skills to do that kind of thing. There's nothing better than word of mouth and when those are successful, very often we get someone else reaching out to us."

Second is product. "It must be exquisite," Barnett says of his product line, noting that the products Patina offers "define who we are." Some lines are chosen for the emotional connection they make with customers. But as important as product is, Patina Gallery is also delivering an experience to the customer. "Sometimes the shopping experience is even more important than the products," Ivan says. "I look at my wife, who is an amazing person with clients, but she's never really selling the product. She's selling the experience and the story."

Creating unique experiences that engage the customer is key to the gallery's marketing strategies. For example, they host events where artists come in and create work right there in the gallery. "We call them 'Observations' that came about from thinking about the power of Cirque de Soleil. What draws people to Cirque de Soleil? Watching amazing talent doing amazing things. So we thought, let's allow people to come in and look at the amazing works in the front of the gallery, but also see the artist in the back of the gallery making the object from scratch. It connects the actual making with the object itself," Ivan says. Not to mention it reinforces the authenticity of art that Patina sells.

Finally, Barnett names "customer experience" as the third factor contributing to Patina's success. "Service still matters," he notes. And Patina's service policy extends to the artists on which Patina's success depends. He sees the gallery's role as being a collaborator with his artists: "We have a very artist-friendly kind of gallery. For example, we are probably one of the only galleries that pay artists every two weeks, through recession and whatever. But when you pay them regularly, you get their best work."

While Patina Gallery is a small, intimate establishment, Ivan manages the business following the best practices of seminal business thinkers like Peter Drucker. "I've had to teach myself business. I'm not a graduate of business school, but when I read his words, there's a classic wisdom that comes with experience."

His extensive study of business has shown Ivan the need to maintain a methodical approach to managing the business, even in the rough times. "From 2008 through 2011, we were just up against challenge after challenge to keep our business in play. That ultimately gets to be the challenge with small business – trying to stay on point and not lose my cool and panic."

So Patina Gallery shares many marketing approaches with such big names as Apple and Tesla. "There's a through-line, from the top to mid-sized to small business to very small [retailers]," Barnett says. "Under their layers, the best companies are doing the same things."

These factors became even more critical after the Great Recession. "Post-2008, the world changed. The need for awareness is so much different," he says. In this way, he says that Patina is doing for the Santa Fe art world what Apple does for computer aficionados. "We put ourselves in that range of doing what we do better than anyone," he says. "We're in the top six in the world doing what we do."

"It's been a slow build, like any devotee brand," he says. He notes that the gallery is continually adding "amazing new items."

"We're keeping up with the new reality; we have to romance the client and then continually repeat it."

Of course, others try to replicate the Patina magic. Barnett tells of competitors that try to imitate, spurring Patina to keep ahead of the game. While these establishments may sell knock-off items, "Patina is selling the original. We are a brand with history that makes a difference."

When Barnett was asked his advice for other small retailers, he, of course, mentioned having passion for the work. But he also points to the need for solid business strategy. "Business plans are still important," he says. "Great ideas need constant strategy."

"It's much easier to open a business than to keep it open," he says. "Know who your competitor is, and know how you're different. You don't want to do this just to have fun," he says. But doing it must be fun, Ivan adds.

Barnett clearly brings a lot of enthusiasm to his work, but it is grounded in a solid understanding of business. "I studied large business strategy for 20 years; I studied what the great minds say," he says. "Those who listened got it; those who didn't aren't around."

Pricing Is All about Enhancing the Value, rather than Marking Down Dollars

Ken Nisch of JGA offers an interesting perspective on the pricing/value equation. Ken says, "People don't necessarily want to spend less. They want to pay less. Lower income people may well be as concerned with paying less as with getting more. But the more upscale customers are just more focused on not spending less, but paying less. So they want to buy the best, and they can afford to pay for the best, but they just want to buy it at the right price. That is why the Costco phenomenon works for these people, but it isn't even on the radar of lower-income people."

Costco is famous for targeting affluent shoppers with deeply discounted luxury goods with selected items from heritage luxury brands. Of course, Ken notes, that a diamond engagement ring from Costco doesn't send the same emotional message as one from Tiffany or Cartier. "For certain things in their [affluent shoppers'] lives, a Costco engagement ring is still not a good idea or roses from Costco on Valentine's Day. If it's for me, I'm all about paying less. If it's for you, I only will pay less if I can get away with it," Ken explains.

That is why a retailer like Tiger Lily with their commitment to the absolutely best flowers can charge what they want, because their customers want, and expect, the best and they are willing to pay for the best. On the other hand, Manny Gonzales gives walk-in shoppers a real incentive to buy – half price all the time, every day on all those absolutely best flowers when they are bought by the stem or the handful.

Explaining the mind behind the madness, Manny says, "Flowers are expensive and people don't know how long they will last. They don't know the difference between a snapdragon and a daffodil. So we take the risk out of it for them. But then three years later, they can't live without flowers in their homes. They become flower fanatics. We got them hooked. So that is where my half-price specials come in. Flowers aren't just for the elite, they are for everybody."

Prairie Edge doesn't have to resort to discounting to sell its unique, handcrafted Native American arts. They simply have to tell the story of how these rare and wonderful items are made and what they mean in order to command a fair and reasonable price for these goods that lets both the store and the artist make a living.

Dan Tribby explains, "We don't draw the elite high-end clients that are common in Santa Fe or New York. We are located in Rapid City after all, but what we do try to do is pay all of our artists, whether they are native or non-native, a fair price for the things they do. We don't do anywhere near a full markup on the items. But what we are able to do is price our Native American artwork from a third or so less than they would find in Santa Fe. The logic behind it is simple. If we raised our retail prices, obviously we would sell fewer pieces over the course of the year and our intent is to sell for each artist as many of his or her pieces as we can, so we can continually reorder. So it may mean a smaller profit for the store, but that is just part of the equation." For Prairie Edge the meaning is in the artwork itself and the prices they charge, while competitive in the marketplace, do not in any way compromise the meaning.

The secret of finding the right price/value relationship is pretty simple if you move beyond the dollars and focus on the meaning, which is the value to the shopper and finding the kind of shopper that responds to your special meaning, who values your unique offerings.

If all they want is the cheapest, i.e., cheap is their meaning, then clearly they aren't going to buy into your particular meaning proposition, but if they value the most beautiful exquisite flowers, the authentic Native American art or a hand-crafted artisan gold and silver necklace or a vintage diamond and ruby engagement ring, then they are going to pay the premium that these special retailers ask. In turn these special retailers give back to their customers by assuring them that they are asking a fair price that is in line with the value that is delivered.

The key to success in the realm of pricing is telling the story around the meaning; the value.

How to Create the Right Price/Value Relationship

Shops that POP! have a carefully constructed pricing strategy based upon offering fair value delivered to the shopper for a reasonable price. That is, they try to maximize the value of the goods offered and price them right.

Pricing is not about how low can you go, but how much value can you offer at a good and fair price to the shopper. Pricing, therefore, hinges upon the value for the shopper, not necessarily the money. The key is communicating with the customer and helping them to understand the meaning behind the price.

Make sure you target the right customers – the ones with discretion.
As we explored in Chapter 5 about affordability, the customer's perception of price is more important than the absolute price. Some people, in fact many people, simply cannot afford to pay $3,000 for an artisan-crafted gold necklace presented by Patina Gallery; indeed some people can't afford to pay $300 for a sterling silver Native American–crafted necklace from Prairie Edge. It is important to recognize that you must target the customers in your community who are able to step up to your counter and actually pay what you are asking them to spend. That is why in today's economy, specialty retailers who offer specialty prod-

ucts need to make sure they are targeting the right customers who can afford to pay and that is the affluent top 20 percent of customers in their communities. Playing to a lower-income customer often is self-defeating since they simply don't have the discretionary income to pay the fair value-based prices you offer. Are you targeting the right customers, the ones with discretion to pay, in your communities?

Give more for less. Customer perception of the value of the items offered is key. By focusing on the value, making that the key to communicating with the customer, you will enhance the perceived value of the item and thus change the conversation to the meaning, not the money. Customers today need to understand what they are paying for, and your role as a retailer is to explain exactly what that is. And what one customer is willing to pay for a hand-crafted piece of artisan jewelry may not mean anything to another, who simply wants to buy a necklace to match an outfit. Learn all that you can about the products and brands that you carry in your store so that you are ready to communicate the value to your customer. And learn about your customers and what they truly value in your store and the shopping experience you provide.

Use discounts judiciously and carefully. With all this talk about enhancing the value, don't mistake the fact that sales and discounts are still a valuable tool in every retailers' arsenal, but it is important to know when and how to use them. As a result, BOGO (buy-one-get-one) offers are often a better choice than offering a comparable 25 percent or 50 percent discount. Limited time sales and promotions are also effective, again if used for special events or occasions. Such programs work to bring customers in and give them the feeling they are getting a bit more for a little less. What special sales and discounts can you offer that will be meaningful and motivating to your customers? How can you give your customers a special something that makes them feel they are getting more for less?

Chapter 14

Create the Ultimate Customer Experience

Make Your Store Immediately Accessible and Nonexclusive

"I don't want my books to exclude anyone, but if they have to, then I would rather they excluded the people who feel they are too smart for them!"

– Nick Hornby, author

Along with all the other features that characterize retail environments that are an ultimate shopping experience – a shop that POPs! – is another critical quality. Shops that POP! are highly accessible, nonexclusive, and totally free from pretension. It is easy to identify stores that express the opposite of these popping qualities because they are inaccessible, exclusive, and give off a pretentious feel; they are profoundly uncomfortable. You don't feel welcome; you don't feel like you belong. On the contrary, you feel like you've got to prove something in order to measure up.

In the October 2014 issue of *Journal of Consumer Research* an article was featured with the provocative title, "Should the Devil Sell Prada? Retail Rejection Increases Aspiring Consumers' Desire for the Brand." Its conclusion might have you believing otherwise, that treating some customers with indifference, even disdain, may increase their desire to buy. But the study's authors Morgan Ward and Darren Dahl carefully chose to use the words "some" and "may," which applies to only some people who shop in the luxury retailing environment. But in today's 140-character Twitter-verse, people will read the headline, skip the details, and decide that haughty and indifferent sales clerks are the answer to the current stagnant retail climate. WRONG!

Fortunately, we read the details of the Ward & Dahl study and can tell you not to believe the headlines. The affluent consumers who are the real consumers of high-end brands and specialty shopping experiences won't stand for anything less than exemplary, caring service. Ward and Dahl didn't study these customers, rather younger people with less money and greater aspirational needs for luxury brands. The real affluent customers don't have aspirational yearning for luxury brands. They believe they are entitled to getting what they want, when they want it.

Unfortunately in the luxury realm, exclusivity is often touted as a quality that luxury brands must aspire to. Our research into the mindset of luxury consumers finds quite the opposite. Exclusivity smacks of elitism. American affluent consumers, a highly democratic lot who truly believe that luxury is for everyone and different for everyone, don't place much value on exclusivity.

After all, exclusivity is all about excluding someone or some group of people. In the luxury realm it traces its roots from the Old World and European aristocracy, where luxury was something that only the rich and titled folks could have. Note also that the European luxury brands are the biggest proponents of exclusivity as a core luxury branding value, which is one reason why many European luxury brands aren't growing as fast in the U.S. market as they do in China or Japan, where such things matter. Exclusivity is more of a turn-off than a turn-on to Americans.

While exclusivity ruffles Americans' feathers, we highly value individuality and uniqueness, so we really don't care whether something is exclusive, so much as we want something that is special and unique and that expresses one's individuality. Americans' quest for individuality is often mistaken for exclusivity. They are very different concepts and they come from different cultural ideals, yet they can appear on the surface as very close indeed.

In distinguishing between the two – exclusivity and individuality – think of the difference between a Do Not Enter sign, which signifies the message of a store that values exclusivity, versus a sign that says Turn Here for a wonderful, personal, individual experience.

The concept of individuality, making your store more special, more personal, more individual for the shopper puts a positive spin on the concept of exclusivity. It implies a similar idea to exclusivity – that the store is a place not for everyone, but for those special people who really can appreciate it – but it does it in a much more welcoming and personal way.

Shops that POP! Make the Customer Feel at Home

Stores that are accessible, nonexclusive, and free from pretensions are simply comfortable, welcoming, nice places to visit. You feel like you belong, as if the store is a place for you, that you are wanted and valued for the time you spend shopping.

We have heard frequently from the shopkeepers interviewed that their customers are like family or really good, close friends. There is a personal relationship between the shopper and the shopkeeper that just can't be faked. The shopkeeper really cares and the shopper knows that and craves the attention.

The home-like atmosphere is a common theme that runs across many of the shops that POP! featured in this book. Many are even set in homes (Godfrey's, Grapevine Farms, Boxwoods) or create home-like settings in more traditional shopping environments. Transforming a store that sells stuff into a "home" where shoppers are treated like real guests, not customers, is one of those paradoxical features that Ken Nisch talked about in Chapter 11 that engages the customers emotionally and evokes curiosity from the individual. They think, "It looks like a home, feels like a home, but sells like a store."

It's by creating that welcome home atmosphere that Pat Burnley and her children and now grandchildren have turned a roadside stand into a thriving retail business that is ranked among the top things to do by TripAdvisor when visiting Lancaster County, Pennsylvania, the home of the Pennsylvania Dutch and the Amish.

Kitchen Kettle Village – From Roadside Stand to a Shopping Village

Back in 1954, homemaker Pat Burnley decided to supplement the family income by cooking up batches of her family's favorite jams and jellies to sell. So she and her husband got a stack of two-gallon kettles and gas burners and set up shop in a two-car garage behind their home where they cooked up the treats that were then sold in a roadside stand. They left the garage doors opened and quickly discovered that people stopped, not only to buy the goods, but to watch the jelly making process as well. Thus a business idea was born that today has grown into a shopping village of more than 40 stores, eateries, lodging with 20 rooms and cottages available for overnight guests, and other activities. Today Kitchen Kettle Village employs 250 people and welcomes nearly 1 million visitors each year.

Kitchen Kettle Village is anchored by the Jam & Relish Kitchen. This is where guests can still watch as the signature Chow Chow relish and Rhubarb Jam, which is celebrated each year in KKV with a spring festival, and other pickles, jams and jellies are made. Another centerpiece of KKV is the Kling House Restaurant, the Burnley's original home, where Pat can frequently be found greeting guests in what was once her living room.

The business of Kitchen Kettle Village grew organically from the original family homestead under the direction of the original family, starting in the early 1960s with the addition of a flower shop and a gift shop. With each successive generation joining the family business, the village evolved in new directions, responding to market forces that present opportunities driven by customer demand, as well as the growing competencies of the family management team.

Michelle Rondienelli, co-owner and president of Kitchen Kettle Foods Inc., and Pat's granddaughter, says, "I don't think our grandparents saw it as a village with over 40 stores and restaurants. For them it was a place to make jams and jellies, have people come and see them make it and serve them cookies along with the jam. Then they needed to make more cookies, so they said 'let's have a bakery.' And one of their friends had a gift shop, so they invited them to join us. With the second generation, my father Mike and his brother Jim and sister Joanne, they looked at what kinds of other stores were needed to round out the village and create more of an experience for the guests. At that time, we were more tenant-focused with our job renting space to other business. Then when my generation came, we saw a great opportunity to put all of our experience and talents to work in developing different store concepts ourselves, rather than bringing in a tenant."

Today about 65 percent of the store operations are family-run, with the remaining operated by independent businesses. The family, therefore, has more control of the overall customer experience and the central concept of providing customers experiences around not only product, but the making of the product, which is an essential part of the Kitchen Kettle Village DNA.

"Seeing how it's made gives people a different feeling about the product, more than if you just pick it off the shelf in a bottle," Michelle says. So visitors to Kitchen Kettle Village can watch the Amish cooks make the products in the Jam & Relish Kitchen, as well as taste the 90 different offerings. They also can see the fudge being made, furniture being crafted, taste freshly-made ice cream and in the Make-a-Friend Workshop, kids and their parents can make their own toys to take home under the guidance of expert wood crafts-men. "That is the heart and soul of Kitchen Kettle Village, seeing how things are made and where they come from," Michelle says.

A recent addition to the family's retail business is the Olive Basin, a taproom selling 40 different olive oils complemented by specialty vinegars. Conceptually it was a fit, being a food product and oil-and-vinegar is not foreign to the business' core pickle busi-ness. But it was also a stretch, as olive oil and balsamic vinegar are hardly mainstays of traditional Pennsylvania Dutch cooking. "It was a category we had to question; are our customers ready for an olive oil and balsamic vinegar tap room? Ultimately we want to feel good about the food we are serving and what people are buying and that was the whole idea about the olive oil business. It isn't just about selling olive oil or vinegar. It's about being able to tell people the health benefits and why it's such a great thing for you. And it is a success, for us and our customers. The key is that we can educate them as to why it is a good product and a good idea," Michelle says.

Creating experiences grounded in the old-fashioned hearth and home values of Lancaster County is what Kitchen Kettle Village is all about. "We wanted to make Kitchen Kettle Village a microcosm of the Lancaster County experience, so guests could come here and experience a taste of everything that Lancaster County has to offer," Michelle says.

She explains what Lancaster County stands for and why so many people come not only from the United States, but all over the world. "It's about sharing the simple life with the rest of the world. People come here and take a deep breath. For an outsider to see our parameter surrounded by the farmland or an Amish man working in the field with his team of horses or to come in and see the Amish women making jams and jellies, refreshes them and gives them a new perspective on life. They come to Lancaster County for food, shopping and the Amish, which is what they can get at Kitchen Kettle Village."

Make the Shopping Experience More Personal Every Way Every Day

When it comes to creating an accessible shopping environment, whether it be a single store or a whole shopping village, it all boils down to sending the powerful message that you are welcome here. Making someone feel welcome is about structuring the interaction in such a way that it meets the other person's needs, targets their wants, and satisfies their expectations.

The more personal and individualistic you can make that interaction, the better. Recall that most of Tiger Lily's business is customized flower arrangements designed to the customers' specifications. But your store doesn't have to create personalized, customized products in order to make your services more specialized and personal for the shopper. However, it does have to deliver unique customized customer experiences working with the products on offer, and as in the case of Kitchen Kettle Village, Prairie Edge, and Patina Gallery, tapping into the unique customer experiences found in the community, whether it be tourist destinations like Lancaster County is for Kitchen Kettle Village, the Black Hills for Prairie Edge, or Santa Fe for Patina Gallery, or just the values that make your home town community special.

How to Make Your Shop Accessible

Shops that POP! have all the qualities we've discussed. They involve and engage the customers. They create curiosity. They are electric, drawing power from within. They have an atmosphere, design, and merchandise that converges to tell a special story to the customer. They are authentic. They offer the right price/value relationship. And they are accessible, non-pretentious, inviting, and welcoming. They give customers the feeling that they have come home.

Shops that POP! know they are good, but rather than resting on their laurels and expecting everybody else to know it too, they are constantly reaching out, drawing people into their web with missionary zeal and self-effacing charm. It is all about making the shopper feel personally welcome.

Draw inspiration from your community. A few years back Unity Marketing did some work with New Zealand Trade & Enterprise. After we made that long trek down under, our host made a special point of telling us she put us up in a hotel in the area where the luxury brand boutiques could be found, knowing my focus on the luxury market. But shopping in a Prada or Gucci store was the last place I wanted to visit. I was keen to experience the uniquely special New Zealand stores and boutiques that expressed its style. While your store may not be located in a tourist destination, there are still special qualities and features that each community has to offer. Make sure your shop expresses and reflects those qualities. What makes your hometown a special place to live, work, and shop? Make sure that your store tells that story.

Less store, more home. Retailing power comes with creating paradoxical shopping environments, those little surprises sprinkled throughout the store that make the customer take notice. Add touches of home to your retail establishment to make the customers feel like it's their home too. Maybe it is flower baskets at the door, a cozy, comfy chair and table, a candle burning to fragrance the store, or incandescent lights replacing or supplementing overhead florescent bulbs. Every shop, even one that doesn't have the advantage of being in a converted home, can become more home like. What can you add to your shop that will give it a "welcome home" feeling?

Staff is key. Your staff can make, or break, the inviting feeling you must impart in your shop, the kind of "I've come back home" feeling you get at Kitchen Kettle Village. Your staff needs to be carefully selected to represent the best of what your special shop is all about. People can be trained in product knowledge, how to run a cash register, or how to post on Facebook, but they can't be trained to be genuinely friendly, even charming. Your staff should be able to strike up a conversation with strangers and make them feel special. Are there staff members in your store that just don't pass the "charm" test? If so, get them off the sales floor and in the back room or suggest their talents are better suited to some other line of work or some other business.

Train your staff to give a special greeting. As we've stressed, retailing is at its core a people, not a product business, so every person-to-person interaction is critical to a retailer's success. People make quick judgments based upon first impressions and you only get one chance to make a first impression. That is with your greeting. The old "may I help you?" needs to be verboten in any shop that POPs! Replace it with something special and unique to your store. Make sure your customers feel like guests in your home, not just a person to whom you may be able to make a sale. What special ways can you welcome guests so they feel like they are truly welcome in your shop, not for the money they might spend, but just for the pleasure of having them there?

PART 3

Putting the POP! Equation to Work

Principles You Can Use to
Make Yours a Shop that POPs!

Chapter 15

Using the POP! Equation to Create the Ultimate Shopping Experience

"In the factory we make cosmetics, but in my stores we sell hope."

—Charles Revson

Now let's pull all the learning from the consumers and insights from retailers together to transform your shop into one that POPs! Here is where we put the ideas, strategies, and tactics to work to create the ultimate shopping experiences for your customers. Let's transform your store from ordinary to extraordinary.

The keyword for retailers is transformation. You must first accept that the continued survival of your store, let alone future success, depends upon your commitment to change, and not just a minor makeover, but true transformation. It means examining everything about your store and its operation and reconfiguring it, not for your personal convenience or operational efficiency, but to put the needs, wants, and desires of the customer first.

The shopper must be the focus of all retailing objectives. Decisions must be made according to what is best for the shopper, not what works best for the store staff. If something doesn't work for or enhance the pleasure of the shopper, then you need to do the hard work to make it best for the shopper. With the shopper going more and more experiential, retailers can't leave anything to chance or miss an opportunity to make shopping in their stores even more fun and delightful.

The Reasons Why Shoppers Shop Have Changed – Retailers Have to Change With Them

All retailers, including the big corporate national retailers and the "mom-and-pops," are equally confounded by the dramatic changes taking place in their businesses. And while the big retailers may have more resources to call upon to manage change, the small independents are out on a limb with little support to see themselves through these challenges. Many small independents blame their problems on competition from big boxes and their favorite solution usually involves a two-pronged approach: beat the big boxes with superior customer service and stock more products that the big boxes don't carry.

! Product differentiation strategy is getting less and less effective – shoppers today can find almost any product almost anywhere. Product alone isn't enough.

The reality, however, is a product differentiation strategy is getting less and less effective, because shoppers today can find almost any product or a perfectly acceptable substitute almost anywhere, most especially from the convenience of their homes via the internet. Product alone isn't enough.

Challenged retailers are getting closer when they see superior customer service as key, and this is where independents have a huge advantage over the "big boys" of retail. But independent retailers need to vastly expand their definition and concept of customer service, take it up more than a few notches into a whole new dimension of serving the customer's desires. From a research perspective, the phrase "customer service" is just too broad and general, like the term "quality" describing products. Both terms lack clarity and precision. They can mean everything and anything, and so ultimately mean nothing.

The idea of good customer service covers such a wide range of experiences and is so personal – what is good for one person might not be good at all for another – that the phrase is rendered virtually meaningless. To take the learning from the research among shoppers and retailers and turn it into strategies for success, retailers need to explore the full scope and dimension of how good customer service at retail must be transformed into an experience for the shopper.

However, the real problem facing retailers today is not competition from better capitalized, better managed, better merchandised, better located, and bigger stores. It is from the changes taking place among shoppers. Customers are demanding more out of the time they spend shopping in stores than just buying some stuff, whether they get it cheap or not. They want payback in terms of more recreation, more entertainment, and lots more fun, because they simply don't need to go to the store anymore to get what they want.

In-store shopping today is a choice, not a necessity. This trend will only continue to be magnified in the future so making shopping fun in your store is the ultimate prescription for success. In the chapters that follow retailers will learn how to put the key POP! Equation to work to make shopping a truly exciting experience.

Review of the Major Research Findings

Before moving to the action steps needed to make your shop POP!, let's review the key findings from the research, because the recommendations that follow are grounded in this research.

Shopper Findings

Whereas need, product features, and affordability influence shoppers, emotions mean the most when shoppers decide to buy.

Shoppers' emotion, how they feel and how they engage in the store, can stimulate their desire to buy, even if their actual need is very low. With emotions stimulated, shoppers interpret certain products and features as that much more desirable and so increase likelihood to purchase. High emotion can make a shopper's budget stretch to afford a particularly high-desire item or conversely if the price is so attractively low and the shopper gets the emotional thrill of finding a bargain, it can stimulate purchase when need and features aren't all that stimulating.

Retailers must play off each of these factors – need, product features and affordability – toward the ultimate goal of getting a shopper to buy. The best way to do that is to attract shoppers by offering a compelling, interesting, engaging, exciting shopping experience.

Self-actualization and personal transformation are shoppers' ultimate desire.

When studying the customers of specialty retailers, one macro, overriding desire emerges as dominant: shoppers buy in order to improve the quality of their lives in some meaningful, measurable way. Shopping in your store, interacting with the staff and merchandise, trying on, picking up, and making a purchase must satisfy this need to improve the quality of their everyday lives.

Psychologist Abraham Maslow defines the ultimate expression of individuals' desire to improve the quality of their lives as self-actualization and personal transformation. Customers' greatest desire is to buy goods and services that in some way offer the prospect of personal transformation, of helping the individual create a new more idealized self.

Retailers must engage their customers on this level, not just people looking to buy more stuff, but people in pursuit of personal transformation and a new more idealized self. The goal then for retailers today is to help their shoppers transform themselves. That will create loyal shoppers who will return to the store again and again, because personal transformation is not a once-and-done thing, it is a perpetual, never-ending process.

Shoppers buy products for the emotional experiences those products promise to deliver.

In this new experiential world of shopping, the role of the product is to stimulate shoppers' emotion and get them to pick up the item, put it in their basket, and take it to the register. It is not the thing itself that people buy, but the promise of how that thing will perform emotionally and experientially for them.

Products *perform* in many different ways, not just in the physical or mechanical realm, but they also are expected to perform on the emotional and experiential level. In the new world of experiential shopping, all products must *do* (i.e., active verb), rather than simply *be* (i.e., passive). So a watch is not just a device worn on the wrist to tell the time, but an item that says who one is and what that individual values. An expensive Rolex watch communicates one self-image, i.e., one has the money to buy such a status symbol of success and affluence, and an IRONMAN Triathlon watch another, that the wearer is an athlete and needs a performance watch.

Expectation of finding good quality products is one of the performance values on which shoppers place a high priority when choosing a store. However, quality is a subjective term, so marketers and retailers have to understand the range of quality dimensions about which their shoppers make judgments and buying decisions. Then they need to make sure that they continue to enhance the quality, adding more and more value where the shopper believes that quality resides.

Finding a bargain gives shoppers an emotional boost.

The affordability hot button, or offering sales and discounts, is the one that national retailers push most aggressively and most consistently today in order to stimulate shoppers to make purchases. The reason that they rely upon cheap price so frequently is that it works like a charm. Even affluent luxury shoppers who can afford to pay full price are powerfully stimulated to buy based upon reduced price.

Shoppers have been trained to expect deeper discounts, so they are discouraged to ever pay full price except in rare circumstances. Retailers need to explore other ways to stimulate the shopper beyond the dumbed-down, 50-percent-off sales approach. Inevitably retailers pay the price in profits from an overstocked selling floor and deep discounts. They need to tap into other emotional drivers, and there are many besides just offering a sale, that stimulate shoppers and get them in the mood to shop and spend money.

Shopper-friendly stores play to the emotions.

Satisfying shoppers' emotional desires, as opposed to their strict product needs, is where specialty retailers' money is to be made. It is tapping into the emotion behind consumer purchases, from the most mundane to the most luxurious, and finding out what is the real emotional desire, not the normal, physical, everyday need.

Specialty retailers' best opportunity can be found by focusing on the shopping experience, not the things or merchandise that they sell. To do this they must transcend the material world, selling things, into a whole new experiential realm, creating experiences. Everything about the store and the shopping experience needs to be designed to enhance the customers' shopping experience and satisfying each shopper's emotional desire.

Shopper-friendly stores become shopping destinations because they truly put the shopper first and foremost in the operations of the store. The store is designed, not necessarily to maximize sales, though that is often the result, but to delight and entice its customers. Stores that are shopper friendly truly care about the customer, not by instituting policies where staff members greet customers by rote, but by employing sales associates who want to take care of and serve customers. The service people must know their products, know the store, and be willing to shop with the customer to make sure they find just what they are longing for.

Retailer Findings

Retailers face big challenges, yet have big advantages over big-box retailers, as shoppers demand new shopping experiences.

Small independent retailers face challenges that, while not unique to small specialty stores, may seem more confounding to them than to better capitalized, professionally staffed, and larger retailers. One of the greatest challenges they face is increased competition, with more stores competing for shoppers' available discretionary funds.

Specialty retailers' advantage is being able to get up close and personal with their shoppers. They have opportunity to rub shoulders with the customer every day, look them in the eye, and learn first hand what it is that makes shoppers smile. National retailers can only read data on a printout.

Use that key competitive advantage to spend as much time as possible on the shop floor and train staff to do the same. Make the shopper, not the shop or what it sells, the center of their work world.

Retailers' primary business challenge is getting more customers and keeping the ones they already have.

Independent retailers say that the number-one business challenge they face is getting more customers and keeping the ones they already have. In their search for new customers, small retailers find that the old solutions, especially advertising in local newspapers, yellow pages, coupon clipper–venues, and other locally targeted media, don't work any longer. They feel they don't have a reliable way to reach out to the potential shopper, tell their story, attract their attention, and draw them into the store to shop. Costs are one limiting factor, but that isn't the crux of the problem. Rather, advertising messages scattered widely across the consumer landscape don't attract shoppers' attention anymore. Retailers are willing to spend money to advertise if it yields results, but traditional channels simply don't deliver any longer.

Because of the challenges of deciding where to advertise and what the advertising message should be, more small retailers are turning to word of mouth advertising as their primary vehicle. However, if stimulating word of mouth is the answer to their advertising challenges, then retailers need to focus on making their shops word of mouth–worthy – or "remarkable" in Seth Godin's terms – and that means making the shopping experience truly exceptional, far beyond expectations, totally unexpected in a delightful way.

Retailers that put the customer first to make shopping an experience share seven distinctive qualities, called the POP! Equation.

Shops that POP!, like the ones that we have profiled here, share a set of specific qualities. The POP! Equation defines the unique way that retailers apply specific strategies and combine them together to create a truly special, extraordinary shopping experience for the customer.

The specific qualities that make up the POP! Equation are:

Involvement Shops that POP! create high levels of customer involvement and interaction. Shoppers do not just want to browse the aisles. Shops that POP! encourage customers to touch, feel, taste, try on, and participate in the store in a more involving way. (Chapter 8)

Curiosity Shops that POP! evoke shopper curiosity and excite the customer to explore and experience all the shop has to offer, from the shop windows and entrance through the different displays. (Chapter 9)

Contagious, Electric Quality   Shops that POP! have a contagious, electric quality that exudes energy. They are so kinetic that even shoppers not all that into the category feel there is something in the store for them. (Chapter 10)

Convergence   Shops that POP! offer atmosphere, store design, and merchandise that converge into a single experience for the customer. The shop presents a comprehensive vision that captures all the tangible and intangible elements. (Chapter 11)

Authenticity   Shops that POP! present an authentic concept. It is far more than just a store selling stuff. It is conceptually driven and reflects a visionary's values. It transcends being just a store into a new realm of experience. (Chapter 12)

Price/value   Shops that POP! have the right price/value proposition. They offer superior value at a reasonable cost. They aim to get the price/value proposition "right," and price their goods neither too high nor too low for the value. Pricing is a powerful communicator to customers of value, and a price that is too outrageously low sends a signal that maybe, after all, the item isn't worth it. (Chapter 13)

Accessibility   Shops that POP! have all the preceding qualities, plus another essential feature – they are immediately accessible to everyone, free from pretensions of exclusivity or snobbishness. (Chapter 14)

What's Next

Shoppers today want more, lots more, than what is typically found in most stores that line the malls, fill up the strip shopping centers, or stand alone as big-box behemoths. Shoppers today want more than just to buy stuff; they want shopping to be a fun, engaging, and delightful experience. Otherwise why waste their increasingly precious time?

❗ Shoppers today want shopping to be fun, engaging, delightful.

The principles that follow describe the ways to transform the retail shopping environment from the ordinary to the extraordinary. The principles are divided by category: people-related, product, pricing, promotion, and place (design) principles. After the discussion of each of the principles, questions and activities are added that spell out specific steps you can take to put these transforming principles to work in your store.

The recommendations are drawn from the research and interviews conducted with retailers who have created wonderful shopping environments that POP! for their shoppers. It may be a bit much to do them all, but your biggest payback from spending time reading this book will come if you take one or more of these powerful principles for transforming your retail store into a shopping experience and put them to work right away. The ultimate survival of your store may be at stake.

Research among shoppers shows many expressing a feeling of profound disappointment about most of the shopping choices they have. They are looking for an alternative that can become a destination for them, a place where they really love to shop, not just a place where they have to go and buy stuff. They want more and the recommendations and principles that follow ensure that you will deliver more to them.

Chapter 16

People Principles
that Transform the Retail Store
into a Shopping Experience

"Dealing with people is probably the biggest problem you face, especially if you are in business. Yes, and that is also true if you are a housewife, architect, or engineer."

—Dale Carnegie

When it comes to retail, people are number one. The emphasis of all retailing strategies and tactics must be directed to influencing the shoppers' behavior through emotion, a purely and exclusively human quality. While other inanimate objects and external factors may play on people's emotions, what most strongly impacts people's emotions and feelings are other people, their reaction, and their own emotions.

In order to achieve maximum success, retailers must manage their shoppers' emotional responses ensuring that their in-store experience is a happy, pleasant, positive, emotionally uplifting one. The single, most important factor in making sure shoppers are emotionally satisfied comes through that uniquely human person-to-person interaction.

! The single, most important factor in making sure people are emotionally satisfied comes through that uniquely human person-to-person interaction.

That is why you must address the people principles first, because retailing all starts with the customers, the people. Every other concern in running a successful retail operation is secondary to the people and that is how a store, no matter what your specific business, what you sell, or what your local competitive environment is, will ultimately succeed: Make the shopper first in your store.

People Principle #1:
Pick Your Profession Carefully

Retailing ranks among the hardest professions one might choose. While many people get drawn into retail because of a passion for a particular product or lifestyle, at its heart retailing is about serving people. If we look across all the successful retailers profiled here, and most especially the small independent retailers, like Mary Carol Garrity from Nell Hill's, Manny Gonzales and Tiger Lily, Barb Emmett with Godfrey's, Kate Collier and Feast!, Rachel Shechtman and STORY, Patricia McLaughlin with Coventry Corners and Dan Belman of Boxwoods, we find first and foremost retailers with a passion for people.

Surely they also have a strong affinity for the products they sell, but what comes across in talking to each of these retailing entrepreneurs is that no matter what business they are in or what products they are selling, from home furnishings to fashion to pet products to plants or flowers or cheese, the most important element to each and every one of them is their connection with other people, and that passion extends to both the customers and their staff.

While Mary Carol Garrity grew up in a family of retail merchants, other retailing entrepreneurs came to retailing from other professions: Manny was in hospitality and food service, Barb was a systems analyst, Kate's background was restaurants and her husband and business partner's was music, Rachel was a management consultant, Patricia was a teacher, and Dan was a business consultant that helped turn around troubled businesses, such as apartment complexes and dry cleaning businesses.

They all recognize that at its core their retail business is a people-business, what they are selling is purely secondary to that. As Dan with his extensive business background says, "It's all business. It doesn't matter if you're selling two-by-fours, as I did as a kid because my dad was in the lumber business, or running a manufacturing company where you're selling widgets, or trying to

! If you are a person who likes the things that you are selling *more* than the people you are selling to, then your retail enterprise is headed for disaster.

help a company build Domino Pizza stores. It is all about people."

An unfortunate fact of the retail business is that there is a relatively low cost of entry, so just about anybody with a minimum of capital can get started in some kind of retail enterprise. That tends to let people into retailing who are totally unsuited for it. As a result, people who really like home decorating open a home furnishings store, or people who like plants open a garden center, or people who like clothes open a fashion boutique, all with the flawed assumption that their primary business focus in retail is around the products they sell. That is a huge mistake.

Mary Carol Garrity of Nell Hill's says, "I have observed a lot of people get into a retail store, like a home accessories store, because they love to decorate. That is a terrible mistake. I got in because I love retail, not because I love to decorate. I'm a people person and that is what I love about retail."

While success at retail does involve some level of product knowledge and expertise, you really can get that product knowledge on the job – and when all else fails, you can fake it. Manny is very modest about the extent of his flower knowledge prior to opening Tiger Lily, as he explains, "I have a secret to share with you. I'd never buy my wife flowers before we opened the shop up. I was one of the most flower-ignorant guys out there. But now I am so excited when I see wonderful things come in. So now we get these fellows who come in – mechanics and electricians – in their big pickup trucks. And they see me as a regular guy who can talk about football and fishing and then get really excited about flowers. And these guys get excited too. In fact, I have one customer who's a boxing coach. He comes in every week to buy flowers. Flowers are awesome. Flowers are for everybody."

So like Manny, anybody can pick up product knowledge on the job, but what you have got to start your retail business with and what you can't ever fake is really caring about your customers.

People Principle #2:
Pick Your Staff Very Carefully

The people you hire to work in your store are there primarily to support the overall objective of the store, which is about taking care of your customers. Your staff members must be as equally people-pleasing and people-oriented as you are. Of course, there are support positions in any business that involve a minimum of people interaction, so their people orientation doesn't have to be as great, but for any staff position that involves customer interaction, you have got to hire someone for his or her people-passion as well. After all, you can train new staff in many of the day-to-day skills and product knowledge that they will need to succeed in the store. But you can't really train a person to be a "people person" – one who thrives on working with and interacting with others. People persons are born, not trained.

! "One of the biggest problems is getting the right people. We definitely hire now on attitude, much more than aptitude."

In discussions with the retailers profiled here, many mention the critically important role hiring the right people for their store plays. For example, Dan Belman of Boxwoods Gardens & Gifts says, "One of the biggest problems is getting the right people. I look at people's résumés, but as a rule, I don't put a lot of weight on them. We definitely hire now on attitude, much more than aptitude. A lot of it is gut feel, but I also ask a few silly questions, like did they ever achieve success in their mother or father's eyes? I have found that people that are striving to please mom and dad have a very good work ethic." This is an interesting observation and one that you might put to work immediately in identifying job candidates who are responsible and willing to make the extra effort it takes to create a truly outstanding shopping experience in a retail store.

Kate Collier at Feast! follows a similar guide to finding the right staff people by looking at personality first. She says, "A lot of it [success] has to do with finding the right person. We've had people that we've tried to train, and sometimes when people aren't just naturally friendly, it's tough to be friendly. We also want people who are really food lovers, but the most important thing in the interviewing process is finding out if they are friendly and do they actually cook."

Rachel Shechtman in STORY is slow and methodical when hiring, because her staff has to service the customers, and be storytellers as well. She explains, "They're the ambassadors . . . and they serve a greater purpose beyond simply selling a product on the floor.

Therefore, we take a lot of care in the hiring of our associates to make sure that they understand the work and expectations at STORY will be different than any other retail job." Given the changing nature of STORY, where new stories featuring entirely new ranges of products are set up regularly, Rachel demands staff members who can really take it as it comes. "We're constantly adapting, changing and growing, so finding a person that doesn't just roll with the punches but anticipates them takes time."

In other words, you have to find people with the right passion; in the case of Feast! it is people who are passionate about other people and food; in the case of STORY, people who can tell stories about a whole range of different products and experiences, and if they have that passion, you can train them about the specifics of everything else. You can't train someone to be truly friendly and caring. That is something you simply can't fake; either you have it or you don't.

People Principle #3:
Pay a Reasonable Wage

If you want to hire minimum people to work in your store, then pay minimum wage. If you want to hire the best people to work with your customers, you better pay them a wage commensurate with their duties and responsibilities. In hiring, just like in every other aspect of commercial life, you get what you pay for. While many national retailers offer generous employment packages including benefits and commissions that give the staff member a real incentive for serving the customer, few small retailers feel they can offer similar programs.

Specialty retailers that have shops that POP! also offer an enticing work environment where people, customers, and staff members alike, enjoy visiting. Tracy Purcell of Grapevine Farms has learned that she can find the ideal employees by drawing upon her customer base. In fact, many of her employees have sought Grapevine Farms out as an employer who offers flexibility and asks for enthusiasm. "We're very flexible; we never force anyone to work when they don't want to," she says, explaining that she would rather someone call in for

! People work for wages and even small retailers need to compete for the best people by offering a competitive wage.

a day off than bring less than their best to the sales floor. "If you're not happy, don't come to work today," she says. This flexibility is part of the reason that Purcell maintains a file of applications from potential employees, many of them current customers, who want to join the Grapevine team. "Employees come to us; we have never put an ad in the newspaper," Tracy explains.

Patricia McLaughlin of Coventry Corners also has found opportunities to recruit new staff members from her customer base. She has gotten to know them as customers, knows that they like the store environment and products, and that offering them an employee discount makes working there especially inviting. Further, Pat gives her staff not just a job, but responsibilities. "I empower our associates. They each have a section of that store that is theirs. They work their sections and want to make it the best in the store. They take pride in their sections," and she might add, take pride in being associated with and part of the Coventry Corners success.

But besides the pleasant work environment, retailers must think about providing extra incentives to their valued employees, including insurance and other benefits, as well as commissions or other monetary rewards for performance. That may require keeping staff lean with you as owners, and managers, picking up more of the slack. But, remember, an owner or manager makes the best use of his or her time in the store working on the sale floor, not in the back room. You can hire people or services to do the bookkeeping, marketing, advertising, website maintenance and social media postings, but as the most important staff resource in your store, you should be attending to the most important thing that will determine your overall success: the customers.

The successful business owners here look at their retail staff as integral to their overall success. They give back to the employees and take responsibility for providing their staff members with a living wage. Dan Tribby, of Prairie Edge, extends their company's fair-trade approach to paying their artists a fair price for their creativity to their sales employees, too. "We take employee involvement more seriously than a lot of other companies do. We really have the feeling that our employees are the driving force in the company." He describes the

> ❗ In hiring, just like in every other aspect of commercial life, you get what you pay for.

company, its staff, its extended network of Native American artists, and its customers as part of the "family."

Boxwoods' Dan Belman uses the exact same phrase, "We keep our employees a long time, and we try to promote a family feel in the business. . . . This feeling we refer to as being part of the Boxwoods' family is hopefully conveyed to our customers, who then feel like friends of the family." These owners express the employer-employee relationship as so much more intimate and personal than a strictly business relationship. Just like family, part of being a member of a family is that you are taken care of.

Of course, paying good wages takes money, so as you achieve more business success, working the POP! Equation, you will generate capital that you can reinvest into the business in order to pay higher salaries and commissions to the staff members who give the extra effort to serve the customers, which makes the business even more successful. What goes around really does come around.

People Principle #4:
A Retailer's Job Is to Be the "Host or Hostess with the Most-est"

Target was onto something when they abandoned the use of the term "customers" or "shoppers" and replaced it with "guests" in their corporate vocabulary. Words have tremendous power. Simply by using the word "guest" to describe the people who come into the store, you create an entirely new way of relating to these people. They become more than just shoppers or customers, they become guests.

In keeping with the guest metaphor, the retail owner's most important role to play is as the host or hostess with the most-est who welcomes the guests into their retail "home." An attentive host is responsible for making the guests feel comfortable, for entertaining them and seeing that everybody has a wonderful time. That is the most important thing the retail business owner or manager can do. You want the people who come into your store to visit to feel like they have happened upon a wonderful exciting party that they can become a part of. For example, Apple Stores have done this through their Genius Bar, which simply draws the growing group of Apple enthusiasts to it like flies to honey.

Mary Carol Garrity has mastered this in her Nell Hill's store where she invites customers to talk to other customers and people feel like the store is an "eight-hour cocktail party without the alcohol." Mary Carol, of course, assumes the vital role of party hostess in her store. She never leaves the floor, but spends virtually all her time with the customers, encouraging conversation, bringing people together, entertaining them, and making them feel welcome. Every day she is hosting a virtual party in her store, and that is one of the secrets to how she has built a thriving destination retail business based upon a customer base most of whom live more than an hour's drive away.

> **!** The retailer needs to think about his or her job as being host or hostess for a new and wonderfully fun party every day.

The best host spends all of his time with the guests and makes those guests the ultimate priority. The best hostess plans for the party up front and has everything ready before the first guest arrives. If the unexpected happens, which it often does, she is ready for it and can work seamlessly around any problem. She spends minimal time attending to the food, but gives most of her attention to the people. That, in a nutshell, is how the retail business owner should work in the store each and every day.

People Principle #5:
Party with the People

The best hosts and hostesses focus on their guests' enjoyment; at the same time, they also make a point of enjoying the party too. In hosting a retail party, therefore, you need to get a charge out of the party you are hosting, and one of the best ways to do that is to actually participate in the joy of shopping with the customers. Shopping is more fun when someone accompanies you who is equally committed to the experience. The very best retail sales people have fun showing customers new things, giving them new ideas, opening up the wonders of the store to each customer. They don't sell to the customer because they don't have to.

The retail salesperson's job is to know the merchandise inside and out and be able to share his or her intimate knowledge with the customer, who can't possibly have the same depth of product knowledge as the salesperson. He or she makes shopping fun by acting as a guide to help the customer explore all the nooks and crannies of the store where wonderful things can be found. Shopping with the guest, rather than trying to sell to the customer, is what a retail host or hostess with the most-est does.

People Principle #6:
Imprint Yourself and Your Store in Shoppers' Memories

"Success is not so much what you are, but rather what you appear to be." —Anonymous

First impressions are powerful and the way people are dressed and the care they take with their personal appearance and grooming send out important messages to those you are meeting for the first time. Because people are the first principle of retail, retailers need to attend to the first impression they and their staff make and be sure it's a positive and memorable one.

That is an important reason why having your staff wear uniforms, either formal smocks or dusters or more informal dress styles, is a good idea. Having staff members dressed in an identifiable uniform can eliminate confusion for customers, so that they know who to approach for help. Such uniforms, whether they are aprons, smocks, caps, lab coats, or slacks and logo T-shirts, should be well designed, clean, and crisp so that they give off a positive, professional impression. In stores where a uniform is not appropriate, consider a dress code. For example, have staff members dress in black and white, to create some level of conformity.

Store owners who greet the customers and spend time with them, should dress more like the customers they want to attract. People feel most comfortable with people who are like themselves, so you want to dress similarly to the customers who shop in your store. You want to be neither too casual nor too formal, but set the right tone for your store and your customers. I find that women generally are more attuned to dressing right for different occasions than men are. However, for you male retailers, especially if women make up an important segment of your shopper base, people notice if you are not well put together. That doesn't mean you have to dress in Italian suits, but well-fitting slacks, a cashmere or silk sweater, and a nice, well-fitted sport coat are never out of style and appropriate almost anywhere. As many shoppers have found, especially when patronizing more upscale stores, they get better service when dressed up, not down. Likewise, retailers need to be attentive to their professional appearance.

One final thought in the style department, adopting some kind of distinctive style statement can be a powerful way to imprint yourself and your store in peoples' memories. It becomes your personal trademark. Maybe your style could be to wear distinctive hats, dramatic costume jewelry, designer scarves, or fun and funky eyeglasses. Celebrities whose fame rests on being recognized know the power of developing a distinctive, trademarked look. So too for you and your store. It is all about finding something that sets you apart; something that people will notice and remember you by, that won't turn people off, but draw people in. Many people are conservative with their personal appearance and individual style. They try to blend in, rather than stand out. But that is a mistake when it comes to running a retail store. You need to make yourself and your store memorable, make a lasting impression; a personal trademarked look can be a valuable asset.

People Principle #7:
Every Customer Interaction Is Market Research

As Peter Drucker says, "The aim of marketing is to know and understand the customer so well that the product or service fits him so that it sells itself." Market research is one of the ways to get that knowledge and understanding. But rather than having to hire a professional market researcher, retailers have a distinct advantage in the research department, because retailers get to rub shoulders with their research subjects (i.e., customers) every day. Mary Carol Garrity of Nell Hill's makes ongoing customer research part of her job, "I love being out on the floor. I love working with my customer. I love listening to what they are asking for and what they are saying. I learn from my customers. Pat McLaughlin of Coventry Corners concurs, "We listen to our customers. They ask for things, so we go out and find those things. What makes us stand out is paying attention to our customers and every detail and every aspect that touches them in everything we do."

Every chance you get to talk to a customer is an opportunity

! Every chance to talk
to a customer is an
opportunity to do your
own market research.

to do your own market research to find out what they like, what they want, what turns them on, what turns them off. You engage them by asking questions about themselves in order to gather valuable business insights that you can use to continue to refine the shopping experience in your store.

In conducting your personal market research, it is important to make notes and record the things you learn. Too frequently valuable insights get forgotten or lost in the day-to-day hubbub. Making a discipline out of recording your research findings, getting your staff members to do the same, and then having the entire store staff share their findings on a regular basis can provide valuable learning. Monthly, maybe even weekly or biweekly, staff meetings to discuss what customers are saying and feeling and experiencing in the store can help identify new opportunities and find new directions for the business.

If you find that the meetings become repetitive and nothing new is coming out of them, then you had better do more market research because you aren't asking the right questions or doing enough research. Your customers are always changing, always moving from what is to what could be. So there is something valuable and new to learn every single day if you engage your customers in the right way. That starts with asking them questions, and probing for how they feel and what they think.

If you uncover any little criticism or negative comment, you'd better perk up and fast. Bill Gates said, "Your most unhappy customers are your greatest source of learning." Too often we focus on the good things our customers say, because that is what we want to hear, and ignore the bad, or worse, argue with them about it. As a rule, people don't want to be critical or say something negative, so when you get even a hint of a negative comment, be attentive and probe to find out what is really going on. Underneath those minor negative comments are serious issues that you can't afford to ignore. Any time you get any passing mention at all critical, pay serious attention to it, and whenever possible make amends to the customer and fix the problem in your store immediately.

People Principle #8:
Know the Customer by Name and Use It

The strict protocol for retail customer service makes it hard to ask for a customer's name upon entering the store, though wouldn't it be nice to learn it first so you can address them by name as they shop. Since it would be more off-putting than inviting upon the first meeting in the store, make it a priority to at least introduce yourself by name, which might elicit their name in return. But once they have made a purchase or subsequently engaged you in a discussion or personal interaction, it is time to make an effort to learn more about them, starting with their name.

When it comes to knowing your customers, creating a customer databases with names, addresses, phone numbers, e-mail addresses, and if possible product, style, or brand preferences is critical. For example, you should ask every customer if they want to be added to an insiders' list to learn about new products that come into the store. Most people who enjoy the shopping experience are likely to sign right up, which can become a powerful resource for targeted promotions and building customer loyalty. Outbound communication can take the form of e-mail, the most cost effective way to communicate today and increasingly viable for consumer marketing, or mail, postcards being the most cost-effective and easiest snail-mail method for routine communications.

Many retailers make a huge mistake by not making it a priority to build their customer database, but that is just letting opportunity walk out your door. We are living in the information age and customer information is one of your most valuable business resources. Just knowing the names of your best customers, the ones who spend the most money, can give you an opportunity to reach out to them to tell them when new shipments arrive or things they are bound to like come into the store. People are busy today and don't have time to regularly browse even their favorite places to shop. Store owners should bridge the gap by reaching out in a targeted fashion to those shoppers they know are most likely to be responsive to their offerings. And that is their existing customer base.

People Principle #9:
Find Excitement Every Day

Shoppers find excitement contagious. They are drawn to stores and shopping experiences that are exciting and stimulating, as Mary Carol Garrity of Nell Hill's describes, "I don't do it for the money. I do it because I love it. For my staff and myself, we are very high energy and very passionate about it. That passion is contagious to my staff and it's contagious to my customers."

The ultimate source of excitement in any store is people: interaction of the customers with staff and the customers with other customers. Excitement doesn't exist in the material things or the physical space, though they contribute to a positive feeling for shoppers and staff. Excitement is something that springs from the individual.

The retail store owner has to find that well of excitement in himself or herself and be prime cheerleader to bring excitement and passion to the staff and the customers. This isn't an easy undertaking, because we all are human. We wake up on the wrong side of the bed, we get depressed, our cat dies, we face daunting personal challenges and defeats, but we can't let our troubles intrude upon our business. You have to put on a happy face on the shop floor and leave your blues in the back room.

> ! The ultimate source of excitement in any store is the people: the interaction of the customers with staff and the customers with other customers.

Serving people, not selling things, is the real business of retail so retailers must focus on the pleasure, joy, and happiness of the customer. Everything else is secondary – and people respond to happy, enthusiastic, and excited people. Each of us is ultimately in control of our emotional responses, so we have no excuse for being less than happy and enthusiastic every day and every way. As Dale Carnegie said, "Happiness doesn't depend on any external conditions; it is governed by our mental attitude."

Putting the People Principles to Work

Here are some questions and activities you can do to put these people principles to work in your store.

Define the three primary objectives of your store. What are your primary goals in having a store where people shop? Make your shoppers the object of each store objective, i.e., my store objective is to deliver to my customers the most extraordinary fashions at good prices.

Among your staff, who is the best working with the customers? What makes them so good working with people? Who doesn't have an easy time developing rapport with customers? Thinking of these employees, what skills, talents, special qualities do they bring to the store? Ask yourself honestly, would they be better off working somewhere else? Would your store be better off without them?

How can you attract more people to work in your store who are like the person who works best with the customers? List some specific strategies to find more people like them, e.g., ask some of your friendliest customers if they would like a job.

Think about the last party you gave or attended. Name things the host or hostess did that made the party successful and the guests feel comfortable and welcome. How can you adapt one or more of these ideas into the operation of your retail store?

Stand in front of a mirror in a typical outfit that you would wear to work in your store. What do you like? What do you think? How do people see you? What could you add, subtract, change to look better? Is there anything distinctive that stands out about your outfit? Is there any style or fashion that you really like that you might not be wearing? Can you find one thing to wear that could become a personal trademark?

Chapter 17

Product Principles
that Transform the Retail Store into a Shopping Experience

"Maybe 3% of the merchandise in the building you can't find within 10 blocks. What's unique about it? Bloomingdale's. There's something about the place that really embraces you."
— Michael Gould, Chairman and CEO, Bloomingdale's

Let's first abandon the notion that product, even exclusive product, can ever be the primary competitive strategy for any retailer in the new experiential shopping landscape. Product, any product, is readily available most anywhere including the world's largest shopping mall accessible through your computer or cell phone. As the above quote shows, Bloomingdale's attracts shoppers to its 59th and Lexington flagship store not because of *what* it sells, but *how* it sells it. It is all about the Bloomingdale's shopping experience itself.

We cannot exclude entirely the overall role of product in attracting shoppers. However, for independent specialty retailers to rest their whole marketing strategy on stocking unique and exclusive products today is to set themselves up for disaster. There is so much product out there available for shoppers to choose from, so many stores that stock either the exact same product or perfectly acceptable substitutes, and it is all too easy to find such product given Google and mobile phones.

Specialty retailers cannot set themselves apart based on unique products anymore. Unfortunately too many retailers still believe they need exclusive products, items that nobody in their immediate neighborhood carries, and hold out for that something extra special, but they are losing sales by not stocking the products that people want, in favor of a search for some illusory unique product.

Today just having exclusive product doesn't get you very far. However, every specialty retailer should strive for uniqueness by bringing in an assortment of different products and putting them together in a unique and personal way that tells stories for your customers. You need to buy and stock new products, not because you are the only store in your neighborhood that carries them, but to present that product in combination with other products in a way that expresses a unique point of view. In other words, retailers need to shift their search for uniqueness from the individual product level to the overall store or department level. That then delivers the kind of product experiences that shoppers crave.

> ! You need to buy and stock products to present a unified vision that expresses a unique point of view.

Take Dayton, Ohio's Dorothy Lane Market. DLM certainly offers unique products: customers will make a special trip for those Killer Brownies or DLM's fresh sushi. But, fundamentally, a grocery store is a grocery store, and most of DLM's products can be found in any area big box grocer. What DLM does so perfectly is lure the customer to the store with those unique products, then keep her there by making her feel special, listened-to, and pampered. The freshly-made lunches, beautiful music, and wine tasting events elevate the experience of buying soda pop and soap pads to restock the pantry.

Product Principle #1:
Merchandise Won't Set Your Store Apart, Rather the Way You Sell it Does

Shoppers want more than just stuff; they want special products that deliver a punch, give a boost, and provide an emotional feeling, and they want to shop in stores that do the same. Too many specialty retailers cling to the mistaken notion that product is their point of difference. How you sell, rather than what you sell, is the true point of difference. A big part of how retailers sell their products is based upon the people principles described in the previous chapter, but there are other aspects that are product specific.

For example, the way you select products to bring into your store is an important part of selling the product. It becomes a part of the entire story, or vision, you are trying to tell your customers through the selection and curating of your store's selection. Each items should link or connect to the whole story. Merchants who do the buying for shops that POP! are guided by clearly defined objectives when they look for merchandise to carry. It is a matter of understanding your customer and why they shop in your store in the first place.

Customers of Kate Collier at Feast! come for the superior quality of food, in particular cheese. So while she has dabbled in other product categories, she has found the secret of success is to stay true to her unique value proposition, "Our main focus is artisanal cheese, so we try to have as many products that are made by hand. So that is our focus on product, it is a combination of small batches, great flavor, and consistent quality," she says.

Kate doesn't just show or display great cheese for her customers, she proves it to them by making tasting a central part of the Feast! experience, "The tastings definitely hook them. That makes them a lot more comfortable to go to the cheese counter. Then as the cheese is being wrapped and labeled, they may see baguettes or slide over to the meat counter. It relaxes them." The Feast! product experience then extends beyond the simple products she sells to the tasting experience that gives the shopper confidence and comfort in buying.

All the shops that POP! profiled here share this bigger picture view of their products, not just as things to buy, but wonderful product experiences to be delivered to the customer. Kitchen Kettle Village invites its shoppers to participate in the Lancaster County experience of a simpler time, one grounded in the agrarian lifestyle of the Amish, and invites them to bring some of that feeling back home in products, from jams and pickles to Amish-made furniture.

"Dog Is Family" is the branding story that Barb Emmett wants to tell through Godfrey's. So she is zealous about finding and selecting the right products to showcase in her store. She selects only the highest quality foods, supplements and accessories that she would confidently serve or use with her own dogs and she makes sure her customers know that.

And as a pure customer service that is all part of the "Dog Is Family" story, she sends out notices whenever any pet food brand is recalled, whether or not Godfrey's carries the brand. If her customers have tainted pet food in their pantry no matter where it came from, she makes it her business to let them know, which only creates a stronger bond with the customers and underscores her commitment to pet health.

The key is to understand the merchandise you sell is special not because the customer can't find it anywhere else, but because of the unique way you sell it, present it, bring it together, and tell a story for the customer.

Product Principle #2:
Create Story-Based Displays throughout the Store

Stories are powerful communicators of meaning and in product selection, it is all about the meaning for the customer. A story-based display is one that uses cross merchandising and brings different products together into a vignette that communicates a message, a concept, or an idea to the consumer. Most retailers do this selectively, in their windows, on end caps, and various other places in the store, but the shops that POP! tell stories with their displays throughout the store, not just in a couple of select places.

Storytelling is what Rachel Shechtman's STORY is all about. She says, "A magazine tells stories between pictures and written words, and we do it through merchandising and events. And our version of publishing is sponsorship." Those sponsors, like Target, American Express, General Electric and Benjamin Moore, are drawn to partner with STORY because they need help on the storytelling part of their business. Rachel and her staff are experts at retail storytelling and these companies need help to elevate their product offerings in that way and sell them with the story.

And your retail stories have to evolve and change, maybe not as often as every six to eight weeks as STORY does, but change they must. Continual rotation of stock has been key for Tracy Purcell at Grapevine Farms, who notes that sometimes she has to move a particular item multiple times before finding the location from which it will sell out. Experimenting with new merchandise and experiences, like a recent cake decorating class, which sold out its first time and may become a regular event, is another reason Grapevine Farms has achieved such customer loyalty and business success.

Through story-based displays, not just lining products up on a shelf, retailers can communicate their product vision to the consumer, so the experience of the store is not product-focused, but story-based. Boxwoods Gardens & Gifts presents a hands-on lesson in telling stories through product displays. Since they don't use traditional store fixtures, they use antique and furniture offerings as a stage for product displays. A shopper can come in, see a lovely hutch with a centerpiece and candlesticks with linens peeking out of the drawers, and buy the entire display for their home. Dan Belman describes their product strategy simply, "We want a fun and friendly shopping experience that showcases unusual one-of-a-kind items and also highlights our creative floral abilities. We use old and antique pieces as our display fixtures, as well as old chandeliers and sconces, all of which are available for purchase. We try to constantly change our merchandise and change our displays based on what new items and plants have arrived, what season it is, and how we can express our creativity."

Nell Hill's is another store where the displays are carefully crafted to tell stories. This demands consistent effort on the part of the store's staff, but it pays off in attracting customers and getting them to buy. Talking about the effectiveness of her store displays, Mary Carol Garrity describes them as her "silent salespeople."

NYC–vintage jeweler Doyle & Doyle has totally reimagined the traditional way jewelry is displayed in the store. Dispensing with industry-standard glass topped counters, Doyle & Doyle displays jewelry in mounted framed cases like a fine work of art hung on the wall at eye level. A customer can walk up to the case and see a necklace hanging at the collar level and imagine herself wearing it. And along with the necklace, she can see other jewelry themed pieces that would coordinate perfectly with it.

Compelling product displays are not exclusive to home furnishings or fashion retail. Take Kermit's Key West Key Lime Shoppe, which brands the ubiquitous signature Key West delicacy through color. Kermit's is a riot of neon yellow and key lime green, with everything from its packaging to its storefront giving a happy, bright, tropical vibe. In fact, Kermit's signature colors are so recognizable that one knows which tourists have been to Kermit's by seeing the neon yellow branding on packaging and bags as visitors walk up and down Duval Street. In a retail climate in which every slice of key lime pie looks pretty much like another, one can easily identify the Kermit's product from its packaging a block away.

Product Principle #3:
Find Daily or Weekly Specials to Showcase Something New

Most shops that POP! tend to look for staff members who are both highly personable and highly engaged in the product category. A winning combination for any retailer is to transmit the enthusiasm staff members have for particular products to the customers in a structured, organized way. Developing a program of daily or weekly specials where staff members are fully versed about just one specific product and encouraged to talk up that exciting new product with customers can be a spark of contagious excitement throughout the store and into the community.

> ! Daily or weekly specials showcasing a specific new product that staff demonstrates for customers can spark contagious excitement throughout the store and out into the community.

Feast! showcases two different cheeses daily, which generates sales and stimulates discussion by giving staff members something that excites them [cheese] to discuss with customers. Tiger Lily has a regular practice of marking down individual flowers by 50 percent and because of the seasonal nature of flowers in the store, Manny Gonzales and his staff always have something new to talk up every single day. And every week Godfrey's has a flash sale for some new dog treat, where Barb Emmett can shine a spotlight on a new brand for her customers to try and they can get the satisfaction of a few bucks saved.

Retailers know that shoppers are always looking for what's new, so a structured, organized program of showcasing something, anything new, can be powerful source of excitement and more sales.

Product Principle #4:
Make it Personal Every Day

There is lots of talk in retailing and marketing circles about the growing trend toward personalization of products. In this day of mass-manufactured products, it is hard to envision an approach to create a one-of-a-kind product to sell. The real opportunity exists at the retail level where the individual sale to one customer is performed. Some linen stores offer customized monogramming. Jewelers engrave. Things Remembered, the specialty gift store chain with 600 stores, bases its whole product strategy on personalizing a wide range of gift items. But there are other ways, besides engraving or monogramming initials, to personalize a product.

Kitchen Kettle Village offers a host of options to create-your-own memories of a visit to take home in the form of a product. One shop, Lily's, offers personalized teddy bears and dolls, a concept not so new with Build-a-Bear Workshops in nearly every mall, but Lily's has a point of difference. They custom embroider a name or message on a bib that the doll or costumed bear wears, with all bear and doll outfits hand sewn by the Lily staff. Another store in the village, Make-a-Friend Workshop, lets kids get in on the action to craft their own wooden toys or authentically dressed Amish dolls from supplies provided on site and under the guidance of a crafts-man. And of course, visitors can pick their own gift assortment of jams, jellies and pickles off the shelf in the Jam & Relish Kitchen.

Virtually every store has some way to customize, i.e., make more personal the products they sell, even if it is just putting individual products together into a customized package designed specifically for a customer's needs. Like Feast!, which offers a wide selection of decorative gift baskets where customers can pick their own gift assortment off the shelves. Or Boxwoods Gardens & Gifts, where you can buy a bowl or other container and the florist center will customize it with plants and plant arrangements.

Customization is a great way to engage customers and make them feel part of your store. Creativity is the guide for retailers to find ways to remanufacture the products they sell in their store into customized, personalized packages. Customers are craving this kind of special treatment and will enthusiastically patronize stores that offer such services. That will also give customers something remarkable to talk up your store with their friends for viral word of mouth marketing.

Product Principle #5:
Keep Trying Something New

One of the things retailers often do as they face increased competitive pressures is to retreat and stop taking chances on product lines that are new or different. They hesitate to try out new lines and tend to opt for products that are safe or have a track record of success. Nobody gets anywhere by playing it safe, though. You have to take chances with something new, different, outside the box. Characteristic of the shop that POP! retailers profiled here is a willingness – even a passion – to stretch beyond their established limits and go out on a limb.

> ! Creativity is the guide for the retailer to find ways to remanufacture the products they sell in their store into customized, personalized packages.

Mary Carol Garrity of Nell Hill's originally founded her store as a gourmet food shop selling coffee and cheese, but every time she went to market she found one new category of goods to try in her store. Every new market meant a new product category until she figured out she could do better selling the new stuff, so she abandoned the food business altogether in favor of gifts and home furnishings. Kate Collier of Feast! tried a similar strategy and moved into gifts, but unlike Mary Carol this was not the best strategy for her local market and her business and she abandoned that expansion model to return to what she does best: cheese.

You will never know until you try something new and you can't judge the success of an expansion effort in your store based upon other people's success. You simply have got to put your toe in the water and take the plunge. Dan Belman of Boxwoods Gardens & Gifts found an entirely new and extremely profitable category in fashion accessories that were way outside his and his partner's comfort zone. Therefore they turned over the buying of the "girlie" stuff to one of their staff with plenty of success to go around.

While Rachel Shechtman makes partnering with major corporate sponsors the platform on which to build themes for new STORY stories, she has also found that showcasing unique and specialty artisan products can add dimension and excitement to the stories she tells for the sponsors. So she has instituted a Pitch Night where entrepreneurs, artisans, and designers can come and make a pitch to become a part of an upcoming story. It's something that just kind grew organically and is now a part of every STORY. "In the same way people pitch magazines to write stories, people can come pitch their products. I've always had a passion and a love for finding and discovering emerging talent, small businesses, new products."

Product Principle #6:
Private Label Is Becoming More Available to Smaller Retailers and a Good Branding Strategy

For years, private label goods seemed to be out of the reach of smaller retailers who couldn't go to the factories in the Orient and buy massive quantities of goods, but today many smaller, largely American-based manufacturers are looking to expand their product lines by private labeling for their clients. From clothing to beauty products to leather goods, made-in-USA manufacturers can develop product lines for you.

Here, in this totally unrepresentative sample of extraordinary retailers, we found three companies that are offering their customers their own store-branded goods. Nell Hill's Mary Carol Garrity is following in the footsteps of Martha Stewart to create a line of her own paints. She is working with a privately owned, U.S.–based paint factory to mix up 20 customized colors. "We have our own line of paint that we just came out with this year. It's real simple, just 20 colors. We worked on it and feel we have the best robin's egg blue, the best red, so we only do that one perfect shade in each color. So we have only one shade of sage green. We keep it simple. And I just keep thinking up new product and new ways to do it."

Feast! too is expanding its branded line of food goods. Their goal is to build the Feast! brand, and private label product is a foundation of that expansion. Kate Collier says, "For the future our goal is to increase the awareness and value of the Feast! brand. We are launching a print catalog and support internet sales where you can order online. We also are creating new food products. One of our biggest hits is our pimento cheese. We also do a selection of dips, spreads, and salad dressings. So we're going to really try and make it a national brand."

And NYC jeweler Doyle & Doyle identified the need to expand its antique and vintage jewelry offerings to fill voids left in the overall product mix. Fortunately Elizabeth Doyle, as a graduate gemologist trained at the Gemological Institute of America, had the right stuff to design the store's own name brand Heritage Collection.

But less-qualified or artistically-gifted retailers can look to other sources for expertly designed, signature store product on Etsy, the global marketplace where craftsmen and customers meet. Since 2010 West Elm, the contemporary home furnishings brand owned by Williams-Sonoma, has partnered with Etsy to feature pop-up shops for Etsy artists in some of its stores. This partnership is going strong, but it seems perfectly adaptable for small specialty retailers as well.

In the future more manufacturing companies are going to offer private label services for retailers that sell on a smaller scale than has traditionally been associated with private label. Key for retailers is to watch for these opportunities and think creatively about the product direction your store's brand can take.

Product Principle #7:
Involve Customers in the Product Creation Process

Customers love to interact with the people who create the products that they admire, an important reason why Ivan Barnett invites his featured artists into the Patina Gallery for "Observation" events where customers can watch the artist at work creating. A recent STORY event was built around artist and illustrator Donald Robertson, which included exclusive Donald-designed merchandise and one-of-a-kind art. And Donald did "drop-ins" where he was onsite to put his personal illustrative touch on products featured in the store.

By seeing the work done to create products, even if they don't have their hands in it, customers become part of the experience. Remember how the Burnleys discovered that people stopping to buy jams and jellies at their roadside stand were fascinated when they saw the big kettles in the garage where the jellies were made.

> ! Seeing the work done to create products invites customers to become part of the experience.

That was the spark that led them to create the Kitchen Kettle Village. And so today the heart of Kitchen Kettle Village remains the Jam & Relish Kitchen, where visitors can watch the cooks, many of them Amish, stir the pots and can the jellies. "We want people to feel good about the food they are buying," says Michelle Rondienelli about the Kitchen Kettle Village shopping experience, where the tastes, smells and sights of cooks using old-fashioned tools in traditional ways to make heartwarming foods remind you of your grandmother working in her kitchen.

If you sell arts and crafts, invite your artisans into the shop to make things on site. If you can't do it in real life, try using video to show how products are made, where they come from, how they are developed.

Product Principle #8:
Be Cutting Edge, Be First on the Block with Something New

Taking a stance to be cutting edge and out there first with new product trends can be a powerful competitive position for any retailer. As we have seen, shoppers are naturally excited about what is new and what is different. Patricia McLaughlin's Coventry Corners has evolved over thirty years of operation from a heavy emphasis on hearth and home with brands like Yankee Candle, to today's emphasis on fashion offerings from Brighton, ALEX AND ANI, and Vera Bradley. "Now it is not about decorating your house so much as decorating your self," Patricia says.

! Being there first with new product trends can be a powerful competitive position for any retailer – shoppers are naturally excited about what is new and different.

Godfrey's–Welcome to Dogdom has a mission to discover the next new trend in the care and feeding of the family's four-legged members. With a lifestyle "Dog Is Family" approach, everything and anything that touches the dog or the family's enjoyment of the dog is within its purview. So Godfrey's business is to uncover the latest products in canine health and safety and bring them to the attention of its customers.

And sometimes what is old can become new again, as is the case of vintage jewelry store Doyle & Doyle. Doyle & Doyle is new in all the ways it matters. It offers a totally new jewelry shopping experience, doing away with the traditional look and feel of a jewelry store to present jewelry in story-themed cases on the wall, like a piece of art, which, in fact, its jewelry is. It is located in a totally new shopping environment, NYC's Meatpacking District, undergoing a transformation from an industrial, blue-collar district to a hip downtown shopping destination. And it sells old jewelry, sourced in grandma's attic, from flea markets and estate sales, in new ways, bringing excitement and vitality to a jewelry segment primed for revival.

Product Principle #9:
Have a Distinctive Point of View and Attitude Reflected in Your Product

"I cannot give you the formula for success, but I can give you the formula for failure, which is – try to please everybody."
—Herbert Bayard Swope

Ultimately the successful retailers profiled in this book all present a unique and distinctive point of view in the products that they sell. Doyle & Doyle presents old jewelry in new ways. Boxwoods Gardens and Gifts offers living floral creations, not run-of-the-mill cut flower arrangements. And Godfrey's–Welcome to Dogdom selects only the best-of-the-best pet products that owner Barb Emmett would happily and confidently feed her pet "kids."'

These retailers know what they are all about, what their customers value, and what they need to do in order to continue to be successful. As we have said repeatedly in this section, product is largely secondary to the people in making a store POP!, yet shoppers want a product experience. Extraordinary retailers deliver that product experience by offering a total vision that is truly distinctive and reflects a personality and vision, often that of the founder.

> **Extraordinary retailers deliver a product experience by offering a total vision that is truly distinctive and reflects a personality and vision.**

Retailing entrepreneurs start their stores with a vision, but sometimes in the challenges of day-to-day operations, they lose some of that vision and get off track. They need to bring it back to the customers and the experiences they deliver. They must keep that passion to create a wonderful, unique experience designed for the pleasure and delight of the customer. Products are only a part of that experience, yet they are ultimately critical to your overall success.

Putting the Product Principles to Work

Go outside your store and look at the products displayed in your store's windows. How long has this selection of products been on display? What does the combination of products say about your store? What story do the products displayed tell to your customers? Be specific in describing the product story on display in terms of what it says about your store and what it says about your customer.

Step inside your store's front door. Describe what you see first? What story does that first thing you see tell your customer about your store? Be specific. Does it match the story told in the window displays? Does it tell another story? Do the stories work together or separately? What three things could you do to the first thing you see to make the inside of your store more inviting, more compelling, and more interesting?

Think about the last totally new product or product line you brought into your store. Think about a product or product line that was totally outside your store's typical product range, such as Boxwoods did by adding fashion accessories into an otherwise home furnishings-type store Where did you display it? How did you decide where to display it? Was this new product introduction successful or a failure? Why? List five things you learned about your customers and what they want or don't want based upon this addition to your store.

Walk around your store and pull together three to five totally different items that in some way or another seem to go together; either they all work together or could be used by a customer together. How can you take these items and make an interesting display near your store's checkout counter? What story do they tell? How can you take these items and make them into a personalized packet or gift package that can be sold separately?

Chapter 18

Pricing Principles
that Transform the Retail Store
into a Shopping Experience

"Goodwill is the one and only asset that competition cannot undersell or destroy."

—Marshall Field

When marketers and retailers think about pricing and pricing strategy, they need to think like their customers, which is about value, not price. They interpret the asking price according to how much it is worth to them. Warren Buffett said it best, "Price is what you pay, value is what you get." The customer's perception of price is directly related to how they perceive value. But the best quality item (an $18,000 Hermes Birkin bag) isn't worth much to the customer or retailer if there is no way to buy what the retailer is offering.

Affordability, whether a customer can afford to pay the price you are asking, is described on a sliding scale, from absolute affordability to relative affordability, which is how much one is willing to stretch their budget to make a purchase. So a customer may look at, admire, and want that Hermes bag, but very few can actually afford to buy it. Then there is an $1,800 Chanel quilted handbag, which is affordable to more people, but still limited to a relatively few affluent shoppers. Or there is a $180 Coach bag, which is affordable to a much broader range of customers, but not everyone who can afford it may actually be willing to spend $180 on it. The perceived value isn't there. Every day shoppers are making these affordability decisions about how much a particular purchase is worth to them personally.

Most people have a price range within which they are willing to spend, with the most affluent consumers having a much wider range than others. Customers can be influenced to spend more along the sliding scale of relative affordability – how much that particular item is worth. Their feelings about a purchase, what it will mean to them, can drive them to spend more than they would prefer to buy something wonderful.

But many retailers, especially mass merchants and discounters, more often tap the emotions of their customers to make purchases they otherwise don't need simply because the price is so outrageously low. People get a thrill from how much money they save.

Because markdowns and discounts work so well in motivating shoppers to purchase, retailers push that emotional hot button often. And because it is so frequently and indiscriminately used, the strategy has virtually trained shoppers not to buy anything at full price, but instead to wait until it goes on sale.

Some retailers like Target and Walmart make a discount strategy work, but that is an incredibly risky proposition for specialty retailers. The fact is, no matter how low you can go in price, another retailer somewhere can go lower.

Remember *Mad Men* Don Draper's advice, "If you don't like what is being said, then change the conversation." When your customer questions you about price, you need to change the conversation to value. This is called a "reframe" in classic marketing. Today many of the best reframes come in the form of stories – stories about where the product is made, with "made in USA" a particularly compelling story. Customers are interested in how the product was made, by hand, by an artist, by a craftsperson; what the product is made from, like rare alpaca wool now that cashmere is so everyday; and how to use it to enhance your life, like the confidence one gets from a stylish handbag or new pair of shoes. While you can explain to the questioning customer that your price reflects the "best quality" for whatever is on offer, you need to back up the "best" claim with facts and figures and most especially stories that prove it to be true.

The fact is discounting and discounters will always be with us.

Their core target market is people who have to shop at discount, which ultimately is a risky consumer segment to target because those who have to shop discount (i.e., lower-income shoppers) have the least amount of money to spend. On the other hand, positioning your specialty retail shopping experience to the more affluent customers is much more powerful and profitable. The more affluent shoppers don't have to shop down-market, but they may well choose to shop there in certain situations. Since specialty retailers can't compete on price against the discounters, they need to focus on the affluent and reframe the pricing discussion around value.

Pricing Principle #1:
Play to Consumers' Passion and Their Desire for Luxury

Shopping provides pleasure, before, during, and after the experience when the shopper takes his or her purchases home. Luxury, at its root, is also all about the pleasure of indulgence. When we talk to affluent consumers about what luxury is, they inevitably define it in terms of creature comforts, those things in life that make it more pleasurable, more enjoyable, more fulfilling.

For retailers, playing to consumers' passion is all about adding luxury value into the shopping experience. It is about positioning your store and the merchandise you carry as being luxurious and special. It is about promising to deliver a more luxurious experience to the shopper, both in the things that you sell and the way that you sell them.

However, in today's new luxury world, which focuses on how the consumer experiences luxury, not the luxurious thing itself, you don't have to pursue a luxury pricing strategy by selling only the most expensive products. Rather, you want to sell things that are distinctive and special, but you don't necessarily want to price them at the highest level or sell only the most exclusive brands. It is about playing to consumers' passion for luxury at a fair and reasonable price.

> ❗ For retailers, playing to consumers' passion is all about adding luxury value into the shopping experience.

We talked about Boxwoods Gardens & Gifts successful testing of handbags in the store. Their selection of handbags looked like handbags you'd expect to sell for $200 to $300 dollars in a department store, but which Boxwoods could sell for around $100. Offering that kind of luxury value at a reasonable price doesn't go unnoticed by luxury shoppers who are in the know about shopping. Dan Belman zealously searches out items that look like they cost more than what he actually has to charge. That strategy pays off, as he shared in the story of a woman who came into Boxwoods and bought twelve handbags as Christmas gifts for her nieces.

Nell Hill's in Atchison, Kansas, follows a similar luxury pricing strategy. She offers more luxury value for less money. Mary Carol Garrity says "Our price is perfect. We have the best price. Our regular price is such a value. It is beautifully displayed, it's wonderful quality, and the value is there because people are always saying 'I can't believe these prices!'"

This is also the ticket for success at Rapid City, South Dakota's, Prairie Edge in their marketing of one-of-a-kind Native American arts and crafts. At Prairie Edge they offer more true artistic value for less than the customer would expect to pay. Furthermore, Dan Tribby explains, this pricing strategy works to bring in customers from all over the world who fly in to buy the artwork they sell for a third to less than half the price found in Native American art hotspots like Santa Fe, New Mexico.

Pricing Principle #2:
Focus on the Meaning, not the Money

If you set out to target the luxury leanings of your customers, then you are playing to shoppers' emotions, delivering to them the feelings of luxury through the products you sell, as well as the environment in which you sell them. For many shoppers getting more for less or finding a bargain is the most powerful emotional motivator of all. Discount retailers look primarily at marking down, cutting prices as low as possible.

If you are playing to the luxury side of retail, whether it is true Luxury with a capital "L" or little, everyday luxuries that make customers feel special, as specialty retailers must, your focus needs to be on the side of giving more to the shopper – in other words, adding more value, rather than simply cutting price. Specialty retailing is about offering products that have added value, more meaning, more wonderfulness while charging a fair and reasonable price, not necessarily cheap, but also not necessarily an exorbitant price.

To be successful in specialty retail with a luxury leaning, think about pricing as a three-to-two ratio: Deliver three times the value over the ordinary product for two times the price of the ordinary one. That means you give the shopper significantly more added value in the products that you sell, but charge them less than they would expect to pay. The focus in this three-to-two pricing strategy is on adding value, not discounting price. You want to give more for less, but not too much less. That is what Boxwoods, Nell Hill's and Prairie Edge do. They focus on adding value to the products they sell and pricing them less than the customer would expect to pay, so they feel good about the price they are asked to pay.

Pricing Principle #3:
Aim for the Premium Price, above Medium but beneath High, on a Scale of Low-Medium-High Prices

In this luxury approach to pricing, the retailer needs to understand the price ranges that exist in the marketplace for comparable types of goods: what are the low-medium-high price ranges that are typical for your customers to see in the stores they shop? In the cosmetic market, for example, the low range of price for lipstick might be under $7; the medium range from $7 to about $15; the high range for the most exclusive brands might be $15 or more. If that is the popular range of prices, specialty retailers should look to offer products that have all the features and benefits of the high-priced brands, priced around $20–$25, but offer these added-value products in the $15–$17 price range, slightly less than the shopper would expect to pay for comparable value.

Pricing becomes a question of finding out what your shoppers would expect to pay for specific products with specific features and then charging them somewhat less than they would expect to pay, but not necessarily a whole lot less. This requires retailers to be very aware of the pricing dynamics in their local markets where their shoppers are most likely to be shopping. New York City shoppers have a totally different perception of prices than St. Louis shoppers, for example. The key is to know your local markets and what shoppers expect to pay for quality, then charge them somewhat less using the three times the value for two times the price rule.

Pricing Principle #4:
Pay Attention to Educating Customers about the Value You Offer

For the discounters, cheap price is all they need to talk about, because that is the main driver in their selling proposition. That being the case, they use shelf tags to display their discounted price and comparable or list price. If you are selling to shoppers' feelings and emotions, you need to play up the value side of the equation and explain how much more value your products offer. Barb Emmett at Godfrey's makes this a core principle for her store, where the high-quality dog food she sells can cost three, four, even five times more than Purina or other mass brands sold at the supermarket. She very clearly competes on value; that the dog is part of the family and should eat food of the same quality as the rest of the family. As a knowledgeable dog parent, Barb has no trouble identifying the best quality food to carry in her store. Price is simply not a factor; quality is. But Barb is successful because she makes the effort to communicate with the customer those specific product features and benefits that add up to better food in the dog bowl at feeding time.

The simple fact is your typical shopper is not as well educated in the value proposition of various product categories as you, the retailer, are. She may be informed and have done her research, but usually you know more. You need to communicate all the many aspects of the value proposition to the customer, so that he or she can fairly and effectively judge the value of the product in her own terms. That, of course, gets back to the people principles we talked about first. Retailing is a people business and the more you know about the people who shop in your store, what they value, what they want, the better able you are to find the products they want at the prices they are willing to pay.

Pricing Principle #5:
Find a Way to Discount without Resorting to Discounting

Offering a discount is different from being a discounter. You can discount some things, some times, without damaging your specialty brand; but it takes clever marketing to get it right. And if you can make that discount program a game or theme it around a special event or occasion, it is even better.

Barb Emmett discovered a cool way to offer her customers a discount tied to a special promotion with a fun twist, called Godfrey Dollars. "They are cute, designed to look like a dollar bill but with Godfrey, the face of the store, where the president's face would be." Barb explained. She happened upon the idea of Godfrey Dollars after an unsuccessful attempt at coupon-clipper style discounting, something many other retailers tried during the recession. But coupon clipping wasn't for her customers, even when she included coupons in her store newsletter. "I am not a coupon business. People didn't even bother to cut them out; they didn't work," she said.

> **!** Communicate all aspects of the value proposition to the customer so that she can judge the value of the product in her own terms.

Then for the store's anniversary celebration, she thought to offer a coupon with a twist. "For every $10 you spent, you got a $1 Godfrey Dollar that you could spend over the next month on any product in the store. I got back almost 50 percent of the Godfrey Dollars. They liked it. It worked, it made sense." So she continued to offer Godfrey Dollars tied with special promotions, such as the "Howloween" Trick or Treat event for Halloween when people dress their dogs in costume, Easter for the annual Egg and Bone hunt, the Thanksgiving-themed Wine and Dine event the Saturday before Thanksgiving where a turkey and cranberry meal is served for dogs. And when customers redeem their Godfrey Dollars, that is a perfect time to ask for the customer's name, address and email address so they can keep posted on upcoming special dog-themed events at the store.

Pricing Principle #6:
Shop the Markets Very Carefully to Find the Maximum Value for the Minimum Price

Post-recession, many of the important trade markets and wholesale shows have found a falloff in attendance. Many specialty retailers are cutting back on the shows they attend and the time they spend at the shows. Also retailers are delaying writing orders at the shows, which doesn't make sense because that is when things are fresh in their minds.

There is no question that attending a buyers' show with thousands of vendors' products on display is a daunting prospect, but the good show shoppers who really work aggressively to see it all and make careful selections have a distinct advantage. They find the treasures among the trash, and can hone in on super value products that they can retail in their store at excellent prices. In other words, good shopping on your part means good shopping for your customers.

Putting the Pricing Principles to Work

Browse your store and find seven regularly-priced products (nothing on sale) that offer your customer a great value at a good price. Take each product and review. Write down what you think the product would retail for in a department store. What is the price difference? How did you find this high value/less costly product? What are you doing to bring each product's high value/ reasonable cost to the attention of the customer?

Browse your store and find three products that you consider high-priced luxuries in your store. What makes these products more expensive than other things that you carry? What special features add value to the product and make them cost more? How do you tell the customer about these added-value features? Take each product and tell the story of why it costs more and is worth it.

Think about the next trade show coming up. How can you find really great products that you can sell for less money than they appear to be worth? What vendors offer great products at reasonable prices? How can you find new vendors that have great price/value products? Plan on spending half a day more at the show than you usually would to hunt new vendors with great products at good prices.

Chapter 19

Promotion Principles
that Transform the Retail Store
into a Shopping Experience

"Half the money I spend on advertising is wasted; the trouble is I don't know which half."

—John Wanamaker

In a recent study of specialty retailers conducted by Unity Marketing, the number one business challenge they face is attracting more customers to their shop and keeping the ones they already have. The problem is that many retailers believe – incorrectly – that the solution to attracting more customers is advertising. Unfortunately, much of the business of advertising is misunderstood, misapplied, and often misused.

The statement above from retailing pioneer John Wanamaker remains as true today as it did in the early part of the last century. Advertising is a far better tool for brand building than building sales. It builds consumer awareness among those people who see and internalize the ad, but it doesn't do much to push the revenue needle. It is something that businesses must invest in at some level, but there are other, better ways that retailers can reach out and grab new customers that don't cost half as much.

Retailers Don't Need *More* Advertising, Just *More Effective* Advertising

A study by Unity Marketing among specialty independent retailers found a large percentage of shops regularly using a wide range of different advertising mediums, including about two-thirds that used newspaper advertising. Those results weren't surprising. What was surprising was how low most advertising choices rated in overall effectiveness, with fewer than 10 percent saying that their newspaper advertising was very effective.

What retailers need is not *more* advertising, but *more effective* advertising and promotion. Word of mouth was used most often by far and rated the most effective, but the question is, are retailers structuring and managing their word of mouth programs or simply leaving it up to chance?

While no other advertising or promotion came close to word of mouth advertising in effectiveness, three others were far and away more effective than all the rest: social media, email, and direct mail. This chart shows the survey results, comparing use to effectiveness. With results like these, it makes it hard to argue for throwing good money after bad by using newspapers, radio, coupon-clipper, Google Ad words, and all the rest.

Rather, retailers need to focus on where they get the most bang for the buck and the greatest return on investment. Clearly, that is word of mouth, social media, email and direct mail. All the rest, in John Wanamaker's words, are the 50 percent (or more) that is wasted.

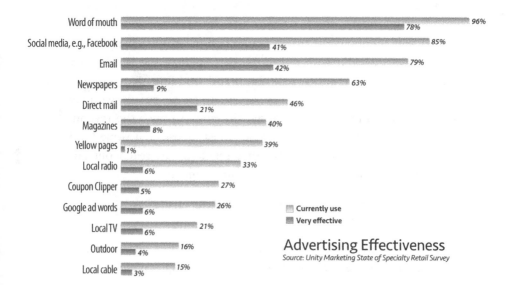

Advertising Effectiveness
Source: Unity Marketing State of Specialty Retail Survey

We've seen that the ultimate solution to attracting more customers and keeping the ones you already have is to align the store, its offerings, its environment, and its service with the expectations of shoppers so that shopping there is fun, not a chore. If the retailing experience in your store is remarkable, as defined by Seth Godin as so special it is worth remarking about to others, then you can build your customer base virally customer-to-customer.

Many of the retailers profiled here have talked about how their businesses have grown through word of mouth when one friend tells another one about the wonderful experience shopping in that store. How else can you explain Nell Hill's building such a dynamic business in Atchison, Kansas, in a town with only 10,000 people? Nell Hill's reached out virally and through word of mouth jumped communities to attract a steady customer base of people who typically drive over an hour to shop in her store. No amount of advertising could have achieved this kind of success.

You must put your money where your mouth is, and that is to invest in making your store a wonderful shopping experience for your customers. Then you need to build awareness and start with some outreach through advertising and promotion to get the ball rolling.

Promotion Principle #1:
Word of Mouth Is Both Your Most Effective Means of Promotion, and the Cheapest, But It Must Be Managed

Word of mouth is low cost and high return, but it must be managed and not left to chance. First you need to make sure that customers have remarkable experiences when shopping in your store – remarkable, in Seth Godin's terms, as worthy of remarking about. The customers' experiences must rise above satisfactory or simply meeting their needs. They must be made exceptional and way beyond satisfactory. This points you back to the people principles we looked at in Chapter 16, because all the great products that deliver exceptional value will only get you so far. You have to excite and stimulate the shopper emotionally and that takes a true and meaningful people connection.

Further, many retailers think the answer to creating strong word of mouth is tied to social media activities. After all, Facebook, Twitter, Instagram and the others are supposed to get people talking and sharing online. But while social media is good and productive in and of itself, it can't be the lynch pin for your store's word of mouth marketing programs. The word of mouth program takes more than expertise on Facebook, Twitter, etc. It requires creativity.

Fortunately there are some very good guide books available to help you get your word of mouth program going and manage it effectively. Some resources to use include Andy Sernovitz's book *Word of Mouth Marketing: How Smart Companies Get People Talking*; George Silverman's *The Secrets of Word-of-Mouth Marketing: How to Trigger Exponential Sales through Runaway Word-of-Mouth*; and Mark Hughes' *BuzzMarketing*. And Arnon Vered wrote *Tell A Friend – Word of Mouth Marketing* especially for small businesses.

Promotion Principle #2:
Expand How You Look at Your Store, Not as a Shop that Sells Certain Types of Things, but as a Shop that Delivers an Experience to the Consumer

One common mistake retailers make that holds them back from reaching their full potential is to define their store in terms of what they sell, which in turn keeps the retailer focused necessarily on the product, and not on the shoppers' experience. In a recent discussion with a fledgling retailer opening her first store, she described her business concept as "a store that sells kitchen cabinets and countertops," i.e., a place to go for those things. But it would be far better to think of her store as a destination for the experiences she delivers to her customers, customized kitchen transformation through fine cabinetry and long-lasting, high-quality countertops.

Those of you who have done any business writing know that passive voice is where the subject of the sentence receives the action, for example, "The boy was stung by the bee." By contrast, active voice is where the subject performs the action, "The bee stung the boy." Passive voice simply makes your writing flat and uninteresting. Active voice, on the other hand, gives vibrancy to the ideas you express and makes your writing come to life.

Describing your store by focusing on what you sell is like using passive voice in your store's description: a store that sells clothes;

a store that sells home entertainment equipment; a store that sells skincare and cosmetics. Each of these is dull and doesn't connect with consumers unless they have a specific need for what you have to sell.

By contrast, an active voice description connects with the consumer's passion and makes the store relevant far beyond selling stuff: a shop where you can discover and express your personal style (Dirt Road Divas); a store within a store where you can create a designer look for your bedroom (Nell Hill's); or a store where floral professionals will create the ultimate flower expressions for your wedding (Tiger Lily).

The lesson for retailers in this new experiential shopping world is simple: Make sure you define the store in terms of the experiences you deliver to the consumer, *not* the thing that you sell. It all comes down to expanding the way you think about your store, what you sell, and what you ultimately do for the customer. Rather than putting the emphasis on the thing that you sell, put the emphasis on the experience that you deliver to the customer. This is something simple and easy to do, but it will be absolutely revolutionary as you shift your focus from the products you sell to the experience you deliver to your customer.

Promotion Principle #3:
Define a Concept for Your Store that Is Your Brand

In my company's research with affluent consumers, we have found three factors that most strongly influence their purchases: brand of the product, brand of the store, and price/value relationship. These factors are all so closely intertwined that you cannot separate them to say that one is more important than another. It is the retailer's branding "triple play." Many retailers tend to emphasize product brands, while they don't really grasp how important their store brand is to the whole shopping experience. Further, they get hung up on price, when value is the key for the customer.

The store brand is the defining concept of what kind of experiences the store ultimately sets out to deliver to the consumer. Each of the retailers profiled here expresses that branding concept clearly and succinctly. It is the founding principle of the store and the roadmap to the future. It is expressed in terms of what the store promises to deliver to the consumer. For Godfrey's the defining branding concept is "Dog Is Family." For Tiger Lily it was to be "the best place to buy awesome flowers," as Manny Gonzales said. For Doyle & Doyle it is to find not the right engagement ring, but the most perfect one, so that the piece you choose speaks to you. The owner explains, "This is why we aim to truly connect with everyone who enters. We endeavor to understand their story and to take them on a journey that is fun and exhilarating, making the selection process a memory unto itself." These defining concepts become the start of the business, its founding principle, and the guiding light for all future growth of the business.

The defining branding concept for a store must be expansive enough to provide room to grow, but concise enough so that the store and its objectives easily and clearly communicate with the shopper. All marketing and promotion materials must clearly communicate the branding concept, as well as all in-store cues and clues that define the store and structure the store experience.

There are whole libraries of great books about branding available through your local bookstore or favorite internet bookseller. Retailers who want to learn more about branding their store should review what is available. You may already have a pretty clear vision of what your store's concept is. All you have to do is write it down, wordsmith it a little bit to refine and hone it, and then make sure it becomes the focus of all marketing and advertising, in-store signage, printed materials, and sales communications with customers. And make sure to use active voice so that the customer is the subject and what experiences you deliver to the customer the verb.

Promotion Principle #4:
Communicate Information that the Customer Needs to Know

One of the biggest failures in advertising is that it focuses on the message that you want the customer to know or what you want the customer to do. Rather your advertising and marketing messages need to focus on information that the customer needs to know or that is most relevant to his or her interests. For example, Manny Gonzales of Tiger Lily, whose branding concept is to deliver the best, most awesome flowers ever, doesn't use his advertising to tell the target customer about how good Tiger Lily is or how beautiful their flowers are. Rather, the focus of Tiger Lily's advertising is the awards they have won in delivering those awesome flowers to customers. Every company's own advertising says they are great, but only one store can claim they won the readers' award for best Charleston florist year after year. That lends the note of authenticity to the advertising and for potential customers who want the very best floral arrangements, that is the information they need to know.

Advertising messages should be relevant to the intended reader. What do your customers value in your shop? In what ways do they connect with your shop? What do other people who are similar to your customers need to know about you to make them aware of your store as an alternative? Manny is on to something when he struts his stuff in his advertising, on the side of his delivery vans, through signage outside and inside the store. He proclaims that people who want the best flowers can feel confident that Tiger Lily will deliver the best, because they win all the awards for best flowers.

Promotion Principle #5:
Use Technology

In the people principles section we talked about the need to record customers' names, addresses, phone numbers, and email addresses. To know who your customers are and to reach out on a regular basis to them is critically important. Every day, every hour national retailers send out a whole stream of messages inviting you into their stores. Often these invitations include a discount offer of some kind, access to a special sale before the general public, or double points for purchases on a loyalty card. But how often do you get an invitation from any of the small specialty retailers where you have shopped, even dropped a significant amount of cash? Probably not that often.

Small retailers make a mistake by not regularly reaching out to their customers with focused, targeted messages, because the best potential customers for your store are your existing customers. You must pay attention to drawing them back in on a regular basis for more pleasurable shopping. It goes without saying that retailers need to record critical contact information about their customers, maybe not for each and every customer that comes into your store, but clearly for any customer who spends more than the average ticket on a single day. Their high level of spending says you connected and made a happy customer who likes what you have to offer, so record that name and use it at least several times a year by sending out invitations, postcards, or email inviting them back for some special event or special sale.

Another serious oversight among many specialty retailers is that they fail to make the leap into the information age and so have not created a store website or used any of the social media platforms to regularly communicate with customers. Let's face it, building and maintaining a website is an intimidating task. Just ask Jodie Robinson of Dirt Road Divas, with its website (www.dirtroaddivasboutiques.com) given a professional polish by design company Dakota & Co using the Squarespace ecommerce platform. It features a clear focus on the kind of experiences that Dirt Road Divas delivers to its customers on its "About" page, and through a carefully curated selection of products and professional photography.

But you don't have to create a stunning customized website like Dirt Road Divas to connect online. Lots of internet host companies offer quick turnaround website creation services through templates that almost anyone can use. Small specialty retailers don't have to go the full monty to include an e-commerce capability where shoppers can actually make purchases online, as Dirt Road Divas does.

Today the internet is replacing the old-fashioned yellow pages as shoppers' primary store-locating tool. Specialty retailers absolutely need to have a basic brochure-type website that describes the store, the branding concept, the scope of the products carried, any brand name products carried, the hours of operation, location, a place to sign up to receive store newsletters, blogs or email blasts, social media links, and any other relevant information that will help the shopper decide to visit your store. And it must be mobile-enabled so that people searching on their phones can find you too.

Once the website is up and running, you can begin to implement email blasts and social media postings to your customers, telling them about new arrivals or other things they would find interesting.

You don't want to overload your customers and fill up their in-box with too much information, but used on a regular basis, weekly, bi-weekly, monthly, whatever makes sense for your store, email is a powerful way to build customer loyalty. But be sure to make those messages focused on communicating valuable information to the customer, news they can use, not just a promotional, self-serving message you want to send.

Promotion Principle #6:
Get Professional Help

Don't be stymied by your lack of technical expertise or graphics experience. The internet tools and platforms are changing so fast that even the technology experts are having trouble keeping up. What is important is that you recognize where you need help, and get the help you need. The internet is far too important in today's world for any retailer to ignore its power, its reach, and its potential. So get started today.

For example, SnapRetail is an online service provider designed especially for independent retailers. It offers a full package of internet services, from website design and social media posting to customer email contact. The beauty of the service is that the SnapRetail folks really understand the needs of small specialty retailers, and the service is priced right for them. Further, the company provides the handholding internet neophytes need to get up and running effectively and efficiently.

Without a doubt there are other internet service providers in your community that can provide the technical expertise and know-how to get your online platform up and running. Talk to your neighbors, visit their websites, scout around to find a website that you like. At the bottom of most any website is a notice of who designed the site or hosts it. Click those links and find the level of support that you need.

Promotion Principle #7:
Exploit the Power of Gifting

Retailers are well aware of the wonderful fourth quarter revenue boost that gift spending gives them, but many don't maximize their gifting sales throughout the rest of the year. They also overlook the marketing power of reaching out to the gift recipient as well. Unity Marketing has thoroughly researched the gifting market and found that shoppers spend about $1 out of every $10 for gifts at the typical stores that fill malls, shopping centers, on main streets, and the big boxes.

While Christmas gifting accounts for roughly half of the typical gifters' annual budget (about $2,000 throughout the year), that leaves another half of the annual spending, or $1,000, for holidays and occasions that happen throughout the rest of the year, with Mother's Day, Valentine's Day, and Father's Day being the most important. Occasions such as birthdays, anniversaries, weddings, and new babies are important as well. However, most retailers don't even think about gifting except for the vital fourth quarter period, or beyond the usual gifting holidays. This is a big oversight because shoppers need good gift ideas and services such as gift wrapping throughout the year.

Retailers need to think of gifting as a unique marketing opportunity to touch and potentially influence two target markets in one transaction – both the gift giver and the gift recipient. For retailers, gifting has all the advantages and the promotional marketing power of sampling and word of mouth, but gifting magnifies and intensifies that power through the unique emotional connection between the giver and the recipient. Because it is "two times two," gifting is exponential marketing.

Thinking about buying a gift is the ultimate in "emotional consumerism," because people use the gifts they give to connect emotionally with the gift recipients. Whenever emotion drives the consumer's shopping behavior, the goal of the shopping experience is not about the thing itself, but the experience. The challenge for retailers, then, is how to enhance the "gifting" experience.

You can offer year-round gift wrapping services, and not just a slap dash wrap job, but give people a selection of expert gift wrapping options from basic at minimal or no cost, to luxury decorator wrap for a suitable fee. However you wrap the gift, it should be carefully packaged so that the recipient has a wonderful experience unwrapping the gift. Internet gift marketer Red Envelope made its overall gift presentation a core value in its branding strategy.

Further, retailers must put some kind of response device into the packages that identifies the place where the gift was bought and that, if they like the item, invites the recipient to patronize the store the next time they need to buy a gift. That could be in the form of a basic greeting card, with identifying information on the back or a well-designed brochure. Take a tip from florists who always identify their shop as the source for the wonderful arrangement it is attached to. The response device shouldn't be intrusive or overly promotional, but it absolutely needs to identify your store as the source for the wonderful gift they just received.

Finally, a really important aspect of the gift shopping experience is the return policy. Gifters value stores that offer generous and easy return policies for gift recipients who want to choose something else. Making your store a pleasant place in which to do returns goes far in building good customer relations.

Putting the promotion Principles to Work

Here are some questions and activities you can do to put these promotion principles to work in your store:

Make a list of all places where you pay to advertise your business, such as local newspaper, telephone yellow pages, website, coupon-clipper magazine. Which of these advertisements bring you the most customers? Write three reasons why that advertising medium works. What could you do to make the other, less productive advertising media work better for your store?

What tag line/description do you use in your printed material/ advertising that describes your store? Write the tag line on a piece of paper. Does the tag line describe what your store sells or the experience your store delivers to the customer? (e.g., a store that sells kitchen cabinets or a store that helps you transform your kitchen) How can you change the tag line or description of your store to focus on the consumer and what your store delivers to the consumer? Think about the difference between selling fashion apparel versus helping customers discover their personal fashion style. Rewrite you store's description to put the customer and what special experience you deliver to the customer first.

Do you have a website? When was the last time it was updated? Do you have a customer database or mailing list? How often is it updated? If you don't have either or both, investigate local web providers about setting up your own store website. Visit the local computer store and check out different software programs that can help retailers build customer databases. Get started today! If you have these services but they are not current, get to work updating the website and/or the customer database. There is no time like the present.

What messages do you want to spread virally by word of mouth? Do you have a formal friend-get-a-friend program for your store? Do you regularly host special events that are suitable for customers to bring their friends? Do you ask your customers to spread the word about your store to their friends and neighbors? Sometimes all you need to do is ask.

Chapter 20

Place Principles
that Transform the Retail Store into a Shopping Experience

"All the world's a stage, and all the men and women merely players."
—William Shakespeare, *As You Like It*

When it comes to the place principles, which refer to the location and design of the store, you need to keep one principle in mind: design your store for the comfort, ease, and enjoyment of your customer. Make the shopper number one in all aspects of design and location and you cannot go wrong.

The importance of place in retail is not unlike the design of a stage setting as a backdrop for a play. The store itself is the stage on which retailers perform their retail "magic." The store must excite the shopper, interest him or her to explore further, and prime the pump so the shopper wants to buy. Both the tangible aspects of store design, such as how the aisles are arranged and merchandise displayed and the intangibles, such as lighting, scent and music, all play a central role in influencing how the shopper feels and ultimately how the shopper acts.

These factors are generally described as "atmospherics" that emotionally impact the shopper including how long the shopper spends in a store, which is directly related to how much money shoppers spend. Careful attention to store design and atmospherics can have a direct impact on the shop's retail performance.

Place Principle #1:
Watch the Traffic Outside Your Door

In this day of growing retail competition along with consumers' changing patterns of shopping, you must be vigilant to watch traffic trends right in front of your store: Is there more or less foot traffic passing by your door? For example, we noted that many shoppers are turning away from big centralized malls as more anchor department stores are being shuttered. That usually results in shops located along the corridors between anchors losing their traffic too.

Retailers often wait too long to address the hard decision about making a move. However, by delaying the inevitable, they end up closing shop altogether rather than moving across town to a more promising location. In waiting too long, their revenues dry up and leave the shop owner with little capital to invest in the costly and time-consuming task of a store move.

You should set up a regular schedule to conduct traffic audits, to avoid waiting too long to discover that your shoppers have moved so you may have to move too. For example, conduct such an audit at least three to four times a year. Pick a day and time, say the third Saturday in the last month of each quarter for a three-hour period, from noon to three, and simply count the number of people passing by your store's door. This kind of traffic audit should be backed up with regular monthly in-store shopper audits, documenting the number of customers actually in the store during a certain set period of time. With this data collected over the course of a year or two, you will have factual and reliable trend information to help determine the direction or change of traffic in and around the store. It may give an early warning of reduced traffic before the results start to be felt in the cash drawer.

Place Principle #2:
Are Your Hours the Right Hours?

Specialty retailers located on main streets often are opened 10 a.m. to 5 or 6 p.m. most days, with an occasional evening thrown in. But many potential shoppers on main street may pass by your store before or after closing time, especially as more people are drawn to restaurants, bars, and pubs in those downtown locations.

It may be the time to think seriously about extending shop hours beyond the traditional 10-to-5 opening times. You have got to be there when the shoppers are there, and if people are flocking to the restaurant down the street when you have already closed shop, your store is missing a huge opportunity for sales. Look around your community, find out when people are there, and be sure your door is open when they are.

Place Principle #3:
A Change in Lighting Can Be a Low Cost Way to Build Sales

The lighting in a store can make a huge difference in how people feel when they shop. A recent survey on atmospherics conducted by Leo J. Shapiro and Associates, found that lighting was the most important element to shoppers in creating a unique store atmosphere, with signage, promotional events, fixtures, flooring, and music following in order of importance. The value of having the right lighting was brought home recently when a specialty retailer shared how a $50 investment in track lighting had doubled sales in the section of her store that she lit up. She was astounded at how strong an impact such a minimal investment in lighting represented.

Too many retail stores overlook the power of lighting and stick with the landlord-provided overhead florescent lights. These are chosen, no doubt, for convenience, but florescent lights are not complementary to colors or people's faces. This may not be a problem in the grocery store, but using florescent lights in a store or a section of a store that sells cosmetics, fashion, home furnishings, and other color-sensitive categories is deadly. Display these products under the same kind of lights they will be used under at home. Today there are so many types of products available for area, accent, and spot lighting that retailers cannot make excuses about not creating the proper lighting effects in their store.

Place Principle #4:
Pay Heed to the Flow of Traffic in Your Store;
Make Shoppers Curious to Discover More

The most popular model today for regulating and directing traffic flow in retail stores is the racetrack model, where shoppers are guided around the perimeter of the store so they can view all the merchandise and departments within the center of the store. While this model might work for large-scale retailers, it is hardly feasible for most small specialty retailers with minimal space or odd configurations.

Grapevine Farms, Godfrey's–Welcome to Dogdom, Boxwoods Gardens & Gifts and Nell Hill's stores have idiosyncratic store layouts that are designed to the shopper's advantage. They are arranged largely in room-sized settings and each room displays a thematic, engaging merchandise assortment. Shoppers are led from room to room, using sight lines to give glimpses of the next room and around the next corner. In setting up these stores, the retailers pay careful attention to drawing the customer's attention through the rest of the store, enticing the shopper to find out what wonders lie ahead.

Retailers might seek out the help of a professional designer with some retail experience to help design intriguing store tableaus that encourage the shopper to explore the full breadth and length of the store. Many retailers will benefit from getting rid of their box or grid-like store arrangement and looking into creating discreet room-like spaces that tell interesting stories for the shopper.

Place Principle #5:
Appeal to All the Senses

We have already mentioned the important role of lighting in store atmospherics, but all other senses can be tapped to create distinctive and emotionally compelling store environments. Encouraging customers to touch and feel the merchandise is one way to do this. While some merchandise must be displayed behind glass, like jewelry and watches, retailers should minimize the use of locked glass cabinets for most merchandise displays. Think outside of the display box, like Doyle & Doyle has done, by presenting rare and expensive jewelry pieces at eye level in framed display cases like a work of art.

People like to touch, and the more merchandise they pick up and touch, the more likely they are to make purchases. The store environment should be designed to encourage shoppers to get up close and personal with the merchandise.

Scent, too, is a powerful emotional stimulant that many retailers can put to use. While burning candles in the store may not be feasible or even legal in your area, there are lots of non-igniting fragrance options, including essential oils, diffusers, and mists. Candle companies report vanilla, lavender, baking scents, and other floral fragrances as their most popular scents, so they are the ones most likely to appeal to everybody.

Music is another mood enhancer, but people's taste in music is so varied and different that your choice of music might be more of a turn-off than a turn-on for certain shoppers. The Leo J. Shapiro and Associates atmospheric study mentioned previously, found that more people (40 percent) said they walked out of a store because of the music, than said they spent more time in a store as a result of the music (22 percent). This is not news to those of us of a certain age, who simply don't think today's contemporary music is music at all, just noise.

But there is a happy medium you can strike with tunes: soft classic rock, even classical music can harmonize with most retail environments and the customers they attract. The key is not to play the music too loudly, so that it overwhelms the shopper. Keep it in the background, but use music as a powerful mood enhancer.

Place Principle #6:
Get Out from Behind the Counter

Architect and retail-design guru Ken Nisch talked about the new way of selling from the ends of the counters, rather than across the counters. By working with customers side-by-side, rather than across the counter which can feel confrontational to the customer, retailers maximize the interaction with customers. This is a revolutionary way to set up the traditional cash wrap station in a specialty store, and one that virtually every retailer can do to enhance the shopping experience for the customer.

The Doyle & Doyle store has implemented this side-by-side approach with its jewelry displays, which helps build connection between the store staff and the customers. Such an arrangement sends a nonverbal message that the sales associate is there to help and assist beside the customer, not create a subtle adversarial or hierarchical feeling like that of a traditional jewelry store where the sales associate stands behind the counter. Doing away with the counters also encourages the staff to mix and mingle, as they don't have a counter to hide behind. They are out there with the shoppers. It enhances the customer experience as well as helps the staff cultivate a relationship with the shopper.

Putting the Place Principles to Work

Interview your store's neighbors about traffic patterns in your shopping area. Do they find traffic is growing, declining, or remaining the same? Are different types of customers shopping in your area? Are people spending more, less, or the same in their stores? How is parking in your area? Work with your store's neighbors to identify three action steps you jointly can take to build foot traffic in your shopping area.

Step outside your store, turn around, and then come back in. What is the logical foot path to take you from the front door to the back of the store? Is anything in your way as you move from the front door to the back of the store? What things do you see? What displays are you missing?

Diagram your store to scale, showing the walkways, product shelves, displays, and so on. (A craft store often has room-arranging diagram kits.) Take your scale diagram and figure out one way to improve traffic flow in your store, perhaps moving one shelf.

Visit five stores in your local area and ask the owner/manager if you can take pictures of their cash wrap station. Try to find different types of retailers than your store. Mount the pictures on a board and borrow one idea from each of the five different cash wrap stations that you can implement in your store. Make the changes to your store's cash wrap station.

Make Your Shop **POP!**

"It is not impossibilities which fill us with the deepest despair, but possibilities which we have failed to realize."
—Robert Mallett

To look at Josh Kilmer-Purcell and Brent Ridge and the company they've built, Beekman 1802, you might think they have been blessed by the gods of good business fortune. Seven years after its founding, they have indeed been blessed, not by accident or luck, but by hard work, diligence and scrupulous attention to detail. You see, Josh and Brent are just like you; they went out on a limb and invested everything they had with no alternative, but to make their business work.

Beekman 1802 was born of necessity. The two were riding high up to 2008, with well-paying jobs in New York City that afforded them the opportunity to buy an historic 60-acre farm in upstate New York for weekend getaways. However, in the same month both men lost those high-paying jobs to the recession and had to figure out how to keep their farm.

"We didn't know what we were going to do," Brent said. "Then a local farmer came to us and said he was losing his place and asked if he could use ours for his herd of goats. So we were faced with no income, a million dollar mortgage, and 80 goats to feed. We started Googling what we could make with goat's milk and the one thing we thought would be easiest to get started in was goats milk soap. We apprenticed with a local soap maker who taught us how to make soap, started using it, and discovered it was amazing for the skin. So that was what we decided to launch with – one product, natural goat's milk soap."

With no plans to open a store, they took their soap to New York City and cold-called on a number of luxury stores on Fifth Avenue and got orders from Takashimaya (since closed) and Henri Bendel. But success had its price. When Anthropologie placed an order for 24,000 bars of soap and the men were still hand wrapping every bar of soap in the hallway of their farmhouse, they had to find a local building with enough space to run their wrapping and shipping operation.

In that new location, they had a small 10 by 20 foot space that could work as a storefront. "We decided if we are going to be here all day wrapping and shipping, we might as well have a little store front where we could sell something if people came in off the street," Brent explains. And so Beekman 1802 Mercantile was born.

From Beekman 1802 Mercantile's Humble Beginnings a Regional Flagship Shopping Destination Grows

Though the Mercantile had humble beginnings, the team had a vision to make the storefront special. "Having worked with Bendel and Anthropologie and having a lot of experience shopping in NYC, we wanted to create an experience that kept the folksy, homespun nature of our company but gave it an urban polish." So with their urban sophisticate style, but still on a limited budget, they crafted tables from aluminum saw horses and rough-hewn planks and installed industrial lighting from Home Depot.

Fast forward to 2016. Winning *The Amazing Race 2012* enabled them to pay off their mortgage. They also were able to invest in buying a property on Main Street in the one-stoplight town that is Sharon Springs. Today's flagship store was established, along with a vibrant internet and media presence that includes publishing, blogs, a reality television show, and appearances on the TV shopping channel Evine. Both Josh and Brent came to entrepreneurship after forging successful careers in media, so media savvy was part of the skill set they brought to their enterprise.

Today's Beekman 1802 Mercantile is an eclectic mix of products, from the brand's own goat's milk products, to home décor, lighting, fashion, and gifts. Brent explains, "Our goal in creating this Mercantile was to create a destination location, a real flagship store, that people visiting the area have to see, like when you are in Vermont, you go to Orvis or in Maine, you go to L.L. Bean."

And the plan was not only to draw visitors to shop in their store, but to bring folks from all over to their village where all their neighbors would benefit. "So much of the community helped us when we were starting out. We didn't know how to run a farm. We didn't know how to make soap. We had to rely on people in our community and that is why community is such an important part of our brand." So important, indeed, that rather than call them customers or guests, as Target famously does, to the Beekman 1802 family those who connect with the brand are called "neighbors." The flagship store has also spawned four "pop-up" shops in Corning and Cooperstown, New York, Manhattan and currently in Boston to bring folks from these cities into their growing community of neighbors.

Brent offers some powerful advice for other retailers starting out like they did a mere seven years ago or for those established retailers eager to grow. First, you have to truly and uniquely distinguish your store. "You have to differentiate yourself in your community and make your place a destination for people with a unique experience and carefully curated products. People are shopping on Amazon, where they can find anything and it's all cheaper. You have to offer something different and in a different way."

Next, Brent says you have to be hungry. "Desperation is the best motivator. We literally had nothing but this property. We had to get it done. Otherwise you are not going to be willing to make the personal sacrifices you need to make to get a business off the ground."

! "Desperation is the best motivator."

The Real Power of Social Media Grows as a "Virtuous Circle"

Finally, the Beekman Boys are uniquely blessed with media experience and social media savvy. They know that the most powerful social media is not what they post on their Facebook or Twitter feeds, but what their growing network of neighbors and friends post on theirs.

"People are craving personal attention, touch and feel and it's fed by social media. That is why we do personal appearances all across the country, so we can have face-to-face interaction with our neighbors. Here is how it works on social media. We post a note on social media that we are doing an appearance and people come out to our event. They get a hug, take a picture, and then post it on their own Facebook page. It's documented on social media and goes in a virtuous circle. All their friends see it and learn that Beekman 1802 is the type of brand where you can go and get a hug."

That "virtuous circle" has done more for the company than hundreds – even thousands – of outbound posts. While NASDAQ calls Beekman 1802 one of the "fastest growing lifestyle brands in the country," Brent bristles at that label. "We think of ours as a 'living brand.' Everything we put out there is inspired by the life we are living." That is the authentic heart and soul of Beekman 1802.

Love Your Customers and They Will Love You Back

In a recent retailer seminar, one of the participants – a more mature man with a long-established business – cried out in absolute frustration, "But what if I don't want to do all these things you are telling me to do? What if I just want to stay like I am?" This man expressed the feelings that were running rampantly, but silently, throughout the entire seminar audience. Everybody felt uncomfortable, put upon, and challenged by the need to change his or her business.

The retailers in the audience knew in their hearts that a dramatic transformation had to occur to keep their retail stores in business, not to mention to make them grow and thrive in the new challenging retailing environment, but the kind of transformation they needed to undertake was a very difficult thing to come to terms with.

Nothing is harder than stepping out into the unknown, moving beyond the way you have done business for years, the store that you have known, that you built, that reflects your dreams and aspirations, and change it into something else.

Well, you really don't have to do it. You can decide that your business is good right where it is, doing what it has always done before, in the same way it has always been done. The downside of that decision, however, may well be closing your doors for good, because the retailing world is changing and your customers are changing and if you don't change with them, you will be left behind.

Smaller Is Better When It Comes to Change

"Dinosaurs had their shot and nature selected them for extinction."
　　　　　—Jeff Goldblum as Dr. Ian Malcolm in *Jurassic Park*

Natural selection doesn't just apply to biology. Natural selection applies in business too. We learn from *Jurassic Park* that the dinosaurs, big behemoths that ravaged their landscape in a never-ending search for food, were selected for extinction while smaller, agile mammals that could adapt, even thrive in the changing environment, survived. So too in business, as we recently have seen thanks to the recession: the inevitable extinction of retailers and retailing concepts that do not evolve as the environment changes.

In retail, small independents have the brightest future and greatest opportunity, because these retailers are agile and quick at bringing true innovation, passion, and drive for excellence to the fore. Their key advantage is flexibility. Small retailers can change on a dime. This isn't to say that big retailers can't change, because they do. However, they are just very slow to make the kind of transformations in their business and their way of doing business that is called for today in retail.

Small, independent retailers, on the other hand, can manage transformation so much easier because every day they are up close and personal with their customers, learning about their desires and feeling their frustrations. Big retailing companies do a lot of things really well, but what they don't do at all well is innovate, and that is what today's consumer environment requires.

> ❗ Big retailing companies do a lot of things really well, but what they don't do well is innovate and that is what today's customer requires.

"When a customer enters my store, forget me. He is king."
　　　　　　　　　　　　　　—John Wanamaker

The future for retailers is to transform the retail experience to focus on the shopper, and what they want and desire in the shopping experience. It is not about selling more stuff to the consumers, although that will be the end result of the transformation to a consumer-centered retailing environment.

It is about expressing real care for the shopper, worrying about his or her comfort, attending to his or her needs and desires, and being personable and personal with the shopper. In a very real sense, you must love your customer, and to do that you have to place them first in the operations of your retail store. The customer will then reward your efforts by loving you back, spending time in your shop, returning again and again, and telling friends about the wonderful shopping experience at your store.

This book has given you the tools you need to start transforming your store from the ordinary into an extraordinary experience for your customer; into a shop that POPs! We have grounded the principles for this transformation with in-depth research about the new experientially driven customer who shops not out of need but desire.

This new shopper is looking for recreation and fun in your store first and foremost, and not so much the stuff you sell. We have explored shopping environments that POP! for their customers – that represent retailing environments that are truly extraordinary, those small, independent specialty stores that play their competitive advantages for all they are worth and beat the retailing "Goliaths" every day. We have defined principles to guide you as you transform your store into a retailing experience around the five key aspects of marketing – Product, Price, Promotion, Place and the missing and most important P, People.

Now our work ends and your hard work begins. Time for us to get back to doing more research and analysis of consumers, their psychology and behavior, and you can get busy transforming your store into a shop that POPs! Good luck to all of you.

Meet the Shops that POP!

Beekman 1802 Mercantile,	187 Main St., Sharon Springs, NY 13459	(518) 284-6039	www.beekman1802.com
Boxwood's Gardens & Gifts	100 E Andrews Dr. NW, Atlanta, GA 30305	(404) 233-3400	https://boxwoodsonline.com
Coventry Corners	Berkshire Mall, 1665 State Hill Rd., Reading, PA 19610	(610) 376-0445	www.coventrycorners.com
Dirt Road Divas	1660 W Lake Houston Pkwy. Kingwood, TX 77339	(281) 360-3482	www.dirtroaddivas boutique.com
Dorothy Lane Market	2710 Far Hills Ave., Dayton, OH 45419	(937) 299-3561	www.dorothylane.com
Doyle & Doyle	412 W 13th St., New York, NY 10014	(212) 677-9991	www.doyledoyle.com
Feast!	416 W Main St., Charlottesville, VA 22903	(434) 244-7800	www.feastvirginia.com
Godfrey's – Welcome to Dogdom	4267 New Holland Rd., Mohnton PA 19540	(610) 777-5755	www.godfreysdogdom.com
Grapevine Farms	2373 State Route 7, Cobleskill, NY 12043	(518) 234-9148	www.grapevinefarms.com
Kermit's Key West Key Lime Shoppe	802 Duval St., Key West, FL 33040	(305) 296-0806	www.keylimeshop.com
Kitchen Kettle Village	3529 Old Philadelphia Pike, Gordonville, PA 17529	(717) 768-8261	www.kitchenkettle.com
Leon & Lulu	96 W 14 Mile Rd., Clawson, MI 48017	(248) 288-3600	www.leonandlulu.com/
Nell Hill's	502 Kansas Ave., Atchison, KS 66002	(913) 367-1523	www.nellhills.com
Patina Gallery	131 W Palace Ave., Santa Fe, NM 87501	(505) 986-3432	www.patina-gallery.com
Prairie Edge Trading Company and Galleries	606 Main St., Rapid City, SD 57701	(605) 342-3086	http://prairieedge.com
STORY	144 10th Ave. at 19th St., New York, NY 10011	(212) 242-4853	http://thisisstory.com
Tiger Lily	131 Spring St., Charleston, SC 29403	(843) 723-2808	www.tigerlilyflorist.com

Afterword

Word-of-mouth marketing is critical for the success of your specialty retail shop. Because managing it effectively is a critical need, here are some ideas to inspire you in your efforts.

How Rock 'n Roll Teaches Everything You Need to Know to Make Word-of-Mouth Marketing Work for Your Small Businesses

In August 2019 the 50th anniversary of the Woodstock Music & Art Fair will be celebrated, a watershed moment for us Baby Boomers in the 60s, when nearly half-a-million young people gathered on a farm in upstate New York for a festival of "Peace and Music."

Woodstock was also notable as one of the early examples of word-of-mouth marketing's power, long before there was internet, cell phones, social media or any other high-tech tools to propel a viral explosion.

With a modest marketing budget, and equally modest goals of attracting some 200,000 concert attendees to the planned three-day event, Woodstock greatly exceeded all expectations, drawing crowds so large that the New York State Thruway was nearly overwhelmed, though it was never "officially" closed as Arlo Guthrie famously said from the stage.

Today we have so many more resources available to spread the word about our businesses, to get people talking and draw them to our special customer experiences. Yet for many small businesses word-of-mouth marketing, while recognized as the most powerful way to market, remains poorly understood, ineffectively managed and sadly too often left up to chance. This got me thinking about the intersection of word-of-mouth marketing and rock 'n roll.

Andy Sernovitz, author, consultant and former CEO of the Word of Mouth Marketing Association, in his highly recommended book *Word of Mouth Marketing,* teaches five basic principles for successfully implementing and managing a word-of-mouth marketing effort. He calls them the "Five Ts of word of mouth."

Talkers: Find people who will talk about you

Topics: Give people a reason to talk

Tools: Help the message spread faster and further

Taking Part: Join the conversation

Tracking: Measure and understand what people are saying

Let's take a look at how rock 'n roll can bring Sernovitz's five Ts of word-of-mouth marketing to life and make it effective for your small retail business. As Bruce Springsteen sang in "No Surrender," "We learned more from a three minute record than we ever learned in school." Let the music inspire you:

TALKERS

By the time we got to Woodstock, we were half-a-million
strong . . . —Joni Mitchell, "Woodstock"

To make word of mouth successful, the first thing needed is to identify those among your network of customers, friends, and fans that will carry your messages forward. You have to know your customers and know them well, which is where small businesses have it all over the big ones.

It is more than just having a database of names and addresses, though too many small business don't even have that. It means talking with people, learning their needs and encouraging them to sync up with you by signing up for your newsletter or blogs, liking you on Facebook, following your Instagram, Pinterest and Twitter posts.

Chances are that the majority of your customers are Facebook users, with Pew Research finding 71 percent of all American adults are using Facebook. And social-media engaged customers rises as age declines, with 90 percent of 18-to-29-year-olds active, as compared with 65 percent of those aged 50–64 years. But even a majority of 'oldsters' are using social media.

TOPICS

Let's give 'em somethin' to talk about, somethin' to talk about . . .

—Bonnie Raitt, "Something to Talk About"

How to "Give 'em somethin' to talk about" is the message that Seth Godin so eloquently focuses on in *The Purple Cow*. You need to do something remarkable, that people will not just notice, but will talk about. And being remarkable isn't necessarily about being remarkable to everybody, but to those special customers who will really appreciate your remarkability and remark on it.

So in our businesses we have to do something truly remarkable, not just making a satisfied customer – too low a bar and boring – but creating a passionate, enthusiastic customer who will take the initiative to spread the word.

It means stepping outside your comfort zone and into your customers' delight zone where they feel you have done something truly, uniquely, personally special for them, which they in turn want to, need to share.

TOOLS

Walk this way! Talk this way!

—Steven Tyler and Joe Perry, Aerosmith, "Walk This Way"

Businesses need to show their customers how to "walk this way" and how to "talk this way" to spread the word. It means providing an easy format through which your delighted customers can easily send it out. A concise and consistent branding platform that is memorable and unique can go far to power word-of-mouth. Don't just be a "gift shop," be the store that does gifts in a brand new way and that talks about that difference in a variety of social-media posts and newsletters that invite sharing.

For example, every morning Beekman 1802, a shop that POPs!, greets it's Facebook "neighbors" with a beautiful picture – some days, several – of the Beekman farm.

The "Beekman Boys," Brent Ridge and Josh Kilmer-Purcell, reject the "lifestyle brand" label, in favor of being a "living brand." Their daily picture postings invite you into their lives and to share their pictures with your friends, not as a strong-armed way to market Beekman 1802, but simply because the pictures are so remarkably beautiful and inspiring. And so the story of their living Beekman 1802 brand goes forward.

TAKING PART

I'm running with the pack . . .
—Paul Rodgers, Bad Company, "Run with the Pack"

Once you got people talking, you must "run with the pack" and participate in the conversation. Thus your word-of-mouth program goes in a "virtuous circle," an endless feedback loop of sending out messages, listening to the messages that come back, then reinforcing the messages with more messages.

It's why Amazon.com asks everyone who places an order to post a review. It's why Brent, Josh or a member of the Beekman 1802 team *always* replies to comments on their Facebook postings.

It's something easy to do, as easy as saying "Thank you" to a customer after a sale, but in a new way and through a new medium.

TRACKING

The answer my friend is blowin' in the wind.
The answer is blowin' in the wind.
                    —Bob Dylan, "Blowin' in the Wind"

And finally the "answer is blowin' in the wind." You have to listen to everything that is being said to you and about you. You have to search blogs and posts, listen carefully to all the feedback coming in and act upon it. As a researcher, I am committed to formal market research methodologies, like surveys and qualitative interviews, but you don't need research training to ask your customers what they think and record what they feel.

Small businesses have a huge advantage in tracking customer input through the regular and frequent face time they get with their customers. But too often, businesses don't have devices in place or the discipline to record what their customers are saying and what they heard.

It can be as simple as keeping a notebook by the cash register to record customer comments or as formal as an annual tracking study to measure customer behavior and preferences; but what is critically important is to put a mechanism in place to track raw customer input and then act upon it.

It's human nature to recall the things we hear that we want to hear, and ignore or conveniently forget that which doesn't conform to our expectations. We can't afford not to make a record of all comments, good, bad, off-the-wall and out-of-the-box, because this is where truly innovative, original ideas for your business can be found.

Activating word-of-mouth marketing is not just a social-media strategy. It's one that should be practiced in every interaction with the customer – face-to-face, online, and on the telephone. Its power to draw new customers to your store can't be underestimated. Make each of these classic rock songs play as the soundtrack in your mind for how to use word-of-mouth marketing to promote your shop and assure that it continues to POP!

Index

About the Authors

Speaker, author, and market researcher **Pamela N. Danziger** is internationally recognized for her expertise on the world's most influential consumers: the American Affluent.

Since founding Unity Marketing in 1992, Pam leads with research to provide brands with actionable insights into the minds of their most profitable customers.

Pam received the Global Luxury Award for top luxury industry achievers from *Harper's Bazaar.* She was named to *Luxury Daily's* Luxury Women to Watch in 2013. She is a member of Jim Blasingame: The Small Business Advocate's Brain Trust and a contributing columnist to *The Robin Report.*

She is the author of five books including her recent mini-book, *What Do HENRYs Want?,* which explores the changing face of America's consumer marketplace. Pam is frequently called on to share new insights with audiences and business leaders all over the world.

Jennifer Patterson Lorenzetti is an independent writer specializing in writing for market research and analysis, industry reports, business and technology coverage, and corporate communications. Her clients include numerous advertising and branding agencies, including EMI Network, Interbrand Design Forum; Healthcare Regional Marketing; Hafenbrack Marketing and Communications, and Nova Creative. She has performed copywriting and advertising strategy work for clients in the retail, healthcare, pharmaceutical, and small business. Her writing has appeared in *Chain Store Age, The College Store, HR Magazine, Human Resource Executive,* and *Private Clubs* magazines.

Lorenzetti teaches several advertising disciplines (including marketing, copywriting, professional communications, and history of advertising) at the School of Advertising Art in Ohio.

Lorenzetti founded Hilltop Communications in 1997, and it has quickly grown to serve clients in many different industries. Prior to founding Hilltop Communications, she earned a Master's degree in higher education administration from Miami University. She is also the author of *Fast, Cheap, and Good: Sustainability, One Choice at a Time* and *Lecture is Not Dead: Ten Tips for Delivering Dynamic Lectures in the College Classroom.*